FIGHTER COUNTRY

The F-14 Tomcats
of NAS Oceana

Dave Parsons and Derek Nelson

Motorbooks International
Publishers & Wholesalers

To the Oceana air and ground crews who keep
the Tomcats flying.

First published in 1992 by Motorbooks
International Publishers & Wholesalers, PO Box 2,
729 Prospect Avenue, Osceola, WI 54020 USA

© Dave Parsons and Derek Nelson, 1992

Library of Congress Cataloging-in-Publication Data

Parsons, Dave.
    Fighter country / Dave Parsons, Derek Nelson.
        p.   cm.
    Includes index.
    ISBN 0-87938-442-5
    1. Naval Air Station Oceana (Va.)—History.
I. Nelson, Derek   II. Title.
VG94.5.N613P37   1992
359.9'47'09755—dc20   92-10972

Printed and bound in Hong Kong

On the front cover: VF-41 Black Aces Tomcats on
strike detachment at NAS Fallon, Nevada. *Bob
Lawson*

On the back cover: Above left, VF-143 Pukin'
Dogs F-14s on formation takeoff from NAS Oceana.
Bruce Trombecky. Center left, Tomcats refuel from
an Air Force tanker as the sun goes down. *Dave
Parsons*. Below left, a pair of VF-14 Tophatters
Tomcats over the ocean near Puerto Rico. *Dave
Parsons*. Above right, a VF-143 CAG bird prepares
to launch from the USS *Eisenhower. Joe Higgins*

On the frontispiece: A VF-32 Swordsmen Tomcat
with a full load of six Phoenix missiles.

On the title page: A Tomcat silhouetted by a
perfect sunset. *Dave Parsons*

Contents

Acknowledgments

As any author will attest, putting a book together isn't easy. The final stages can be downright nightmarish despite an interesting topic. The tedious and frustrating chore of completing the book is offset by the dozens of rewarding contacts and relationships that result during the project's research stage. This book is the product of the collective contributions of many individuals whom we'd like to thank.

Captain Hugh Winters, USN (ret.), one of the first aviators to drag a tailwheel through the grassy overrun at the fledgling field at Oceana was a generous contributor of his time and recollections about those early days. NAS Oceana Public Affairs Officer (PAO) "Ace" Ewers and his assistant Annette Hall were enthusiastic supporters and provided invaluable rare photographs of Oceana in its infancy. Equally enthusiastic was Lieutenant Cathy Davis, Fighter Wing 1 PAO, who cheerfully cooperated in every way possible.

Crucial to this book are the images that tell the visual story of Oceana and its fighter squadrons. Joe Leo's masterful eye and gift for capturing subtle color provided many images unavailable in official archives. Bruce Trombecky's admirable dedication in devoting endless hours camped out between Oceana's runways produced some of the most striking images of Fighter Wing 1 aircraft. Bob Lawson continued to be a valued friend, critic, advisor, and photographer without equal.

A number of active duty aircrew made significant contributions to documenting Tomcats in action. One of the most productive and talented aerial photographers is Commander John Leenhouts whose Tomcat images were welcome additions to this book. Lieutenant Commander Ken Neubauer's work while assigned to VF-33 provided varied and striking photos of Starfighters in action. A relative newcomer showing tremendous talent is Lieutenant Gerry Parsons who recorded some of the most unique photographs of the VF-41 Black Aces during Operation Desert Storm. The practiced eye of Lieutenant Commander Dana Potts produced enduring and classic views of Tomcats throughout his time at Oceana. The best images to ever come out of the VF-142 Ghostriders were thanks to the efforts of Lieutenant Mike Silva while the VF-143 Pukin' Dogs were equally well-chronicled by Joe Higgins. Petty Officers Falkenheiner, Lipski, and Moore of the USS *Kennedy*'s photo lab were each super photographers in their own right and valued friends and associates. The visual chronicle of life at sea could not have been told adequately without the imaginative and extensive work of Lieutenant Max Dugan. Lieutenant Commander Ray Tranchant was also extremely helpful and very generous in sharing his photo collection.

A tremendous amount of thanks is due to the News Photo Division of the Navy Office of Information. Under the direction of Russ Egnor, the Navy's collection of current imagery has been completely revamped and revitalized. During Desert Storm, both Russ and his able assistant Pat Toombs expertly solicited, pro-

A VF-101 Challengers Kfir flies formation with a VF-101 Grim Reapers Tomcat. VF-101 is the East Coast fleet replenishment squadron—formerly called replacement air group and still known as the RAG—which trains aircrews prior to their assignment to fleet squadrons. In the RAG, aircrews are trained in dissimilar air combat maneuvering by flying against aircraft such as the A-4 Skyhawk, F-5 Tiger, or F-16N Falcon (Kfirs are no longer used). *Dana Potts*

A rare camouflaged VF-103 Sluggers Tomcat. While assigned to TOPGUN, Tomcat aircrews sometimes camouflage their aircraft with water-based paint to gain some parity with the well-camouflaged adversary birds flown by the TOPGUN instructors. *Dana Potts*

cured, and managed the best imagery available from naval units.

The reflections, experiences, and musings of many aviators were especially helpful in completing the book's textual portions. Captain Tom Hudner, Jr., USN (ret.), gave an illuminating and powerfully moving account of his attempt to save Ensign Jesse Brown on Korea's frigid snow-covered slopes, which earned him the Medal of Honor. Lieutenant Ward Carroll's incomparable imagination and wit were especially refreshing; it is very pleasing to have some of his work incorporated in the text. Captain Tom MacKenzie provided unique insight into the Pukin' Dogs' history and legacy as did Captain Bob Dickerson. The always colorfully told tales of Commander Roy Gordon concerning the days of the Phantom and VF-171 Key West ACM detachment were very valuable as were the accounts of Commander Jack Andrews, USN (ret.), and his days flying F4D Skyrays with VF-74. The arrival of the F-4 Phantom at Oceana and its fleet introduction could not have been told without the perspective of Captain Gerald O'Rourke, USN (ret.). Captain Hugh Callan, USN (ret.), was very helpful and generous with his stories of moving VF-102 and its F4D Skyrays from NAS Cecil to NAS Oceana.

Several fellow authors rendered invaluable support through their encouragement, sharing of resources, and friendship. Peter Mersky, a noted historian and photographer, was considerably helpful from start to finish. Barrett Tillman's incomparable knowledge of both World War II and "living" sources of information as well as his outstanding book series on the Hellcat, Wildcat, and Corsair were indispensable. Bob Dorr was extremely helpful in sharing photography, research material, and lessons learned from his prolific writing career. The writing and shooting team of Al and Freida Landau were always willing to help in any way. Other fellow authors who shared information and were great counsel include Norman Polmar, Jeff Ethell, Dick Hallion, Tim Wooldridge, "Zip" Rausa, Mark Meyer, Lon Nordeen, George Hall, and John Elliot.

A special mention needs to be made of the enormous contribution that *The Hook* and *Approach* magazines have made not only to this book, but to the preserving and sharing of experiences and accomplishments of carrier aviation. During his tenure as editor (and creator) of *The Hook*, Bob Lawson gathered the very best of tailhook aviation's images, history, and current events, which served as a major source for this book. *Approach* mirrors *The Hook*'s stature as the best magazine of its kind by presenting exciting first-person narratives of carrier aviators' experiences, which have maintained such strong reader loyalty (even in the Air Force) over the years and of which several are included in the text.

A number of relatives deserve special mention: Shirley Parsons, a career school teacher and staunch aviation supporter, encouraged my reading at an early age and fed my aviation book habit for thirty years. Elizabeth Allen whose companionship and hospitality during my Washington days were so supportive during the sprint to finish the project. My younger sister, Nancy, who took the time to read and provide a layperson's perspective on the text as well as being a super friend and supporter. Harry, Helen, and Bill Hawver, my wife's family, always showed genuine interest in all my writing and were so understanding when I missed family events because I was chained to a computer and a deadline. My own parents, Frank and Barbara Parsons, nurtured my love for aviation from the start, especially Dad, who started my library, continues to contribute to it, and generously shared his camera equipment and books.

Final thanks are due to the women in my life, Kathryn, Amanda, and Alexandra, who were always understanding over the past few years it took to complete this project. They were particularly supportive even when the book robbed them of shared time as a family, which the Navy was already so expert in doing. Kathy, my wife: no more books and mess . . . for a while. Mandy and Alex, thanks for staying out of my book stuff; we can go driving and play games now.

One more final note of thanks: This book would have never become a reality if not for the dogged determination and expertise of our editor, Greg Field. He was crucial to bringing this book to press and his endless patience throughout significant delays, notably Desert Storm, which occupied the full attention of the principal author for the better part of a year while the manuscript was in the critical final writing stage. Greg: thanks, you've been a valued friend and editor through it all.

Chapter 1

Naval Air Station Oceana

Naval Air Station (NAS) Oceana's rise from swampy wasteland began in 1940. That year the Navy decided to construct additional airfields in the Hampton Roads, Virginia, area in anticipation of wartime needs. The Naval Air Center, Hampton Roads, had been long established and featured a mature airfield with first-class piers nearby for the Atlantic fleet aircraft carriers. With war clouds looming on the horizon for the United States, and Europe already embroiled in war, naval aviation was about to undergo a tremendous expansion to meet the needs of war. That meant more airfields. The Naval Air Center had reached its growth potential so the Bureau of Aeronautics sent a survey team to locate sites for the construction of small airfields that were in close proximity to the Naval Air Center. A suitable site was found near the small town of Oceana. Oceana was barely on the map and, up until this time, seemed to have no future. The lands around Oceana were wet lowlands that flooded and were not viewed as having any potential. At the time, a single road connected the resort town of Virginia Beach with Norfolk. On November 25, 1940, the federal government purchased 325.8 acres for construction of an airfield that was designated Outlying Landing Field Oceana.

Plankowners

Construction began that December on two 2,500-foot sand-asphalt runways, which were completed a year later. In 1942, Fighting Squadron 9 drew the honor of being the first tenants to arrive. Commanded by Lieutenant Commander Jack Raby, and equipped with F4F-3 Wildcats, VF-9 had the field virtually to themselves. Of course, there wasn't much there to have to themselves. The original field had only a single wooden building that served as an ambulance garage and caretaker's quarters. The squadron arrived as workers were upgrading the field to handle squadrons as permanent tenants. The field had a modest tower with radios that sometimes worked, fuel via truck, and "facilities" for thirty-two officers and 172 enlisted men—just slightly more than a squadron complement. The field became home to the men of VF-9 along with one chief petty officer and twelve men assigned to the field to care for the station equipment, such as it was. A couple of Quonset huts served as quarters for the bachelors and troops. The squadron members had to build their own officer's club from leftover materials. When it rained, the few buildings that did exist were islands in a sea of mud, but they were home.

Fighter squadrons based at the Naval Air Center's Chambers Field didn't quite mix in with the flag (admiral's) presence there, especially the non-aviator types. The atmosphere was too stifling for a typical fighter squadron and conversely, the senior officers (both aviation and surface) found fighter squadron behavior a bit on the wild side. The outlying airfield expansion seemed to suit both parties well. Lieutenant Commander Tom Blackburn, Commanding Officer (CO) of Escort Fighter Squadron 29 (VGF-29), had a snootful of being in the armpit of the brass since commissioning

The Fighter Wing 1 shoulder patch. Left, two VF-143 Tomcats make a formation takeoff from NAS Oceana. *Bruce Trombecky*

These buildings are representative of the early structures built in the 1940s at Oceana. By the late 1950s, they were in poor condition as evidenced here. Below, Curtiss SB2C Helldivers fly over Oceana during World War II. *US Navy*

VGF-29 in July 1942 at Norfolk. When his unit moved to an outlying field, he was overjoyed to escape, as he put it, the "complications and strictures of a big-time base like NAS Norfolk." VGF-29 moved almost next door to VF-9 at nearby Naval Auxiliary Air Station (NAAS) Pungo, which was also in the boondocks, but, like VF-9, had the field to itself.

Both squadrons began intensive workups for impending combat deployments. VF-9 was formed as part of the *Essex* air group, but when *Essex* wasn't ready in time, VF-9 was tapped to join VF-41 in USS *Ranger* for an October deployment as part of Operation Torch, the invasion of North Africa. VGF-29 went along in USS *Santee*. All three squadrons distinguished themselves. VF-9 saw action against Vichy French aircraft over North Africa, resulting in six confirmed victories.

Field with a Future

By the time the squadrons returned to what VF-9 executive officer Lieutenant Hugh Winters called their "happy nest" in early December 1942, workers were upgrading the field

An F6F Hellcat and an SNJ trainer parked in front of the large hangars constructed on the original north side of the field. Below, the original hangar and tower complex at North Field. This structure served the field well into the 1950s. *US Navy*

to a naval auxiliary air station. Officials had allocated $3 million for expanding the facilities to handle more aircraft and personnel and for lengthening the runways. The squadron had been scheduled to transition to the new F4U Corsair after their return, but production delays resulted in their receiving the first F6F-3 Hellcats to be assigned to a fleet squadron. The first Hellcats were picked by squadron pilots at the factory and ferried to Oceana on January 16, 1943. VF-9 then began familiarizing themselves with the Hellcat in preparation for taking it into combat. *Essex* was finally commissioned on December 31, 1942, and VF-9 was slated to join her for their combat deployment.

Farewell to VF-9

By summer, both squadron and ship were ready for deployment and *Essex* sailed for the Pacific with VF-9 aboard. After arriving in Hawaii, Lieutenant Winters was chagrined to get unexpected orders off the ship to form and command a new F6F squadron, VF-19, at NAS Los Alamitos, California. Lieutenant Com-

mander Raby was due to roll shortly and Winters had expected to fleet up to CO of VF-9, after having had such a personal hand in shaping the unit. Lieutenant Phil Torrey moved into the executive officer slot upon Winters' departure and took command just prior to the first combat in August. In August, VF-9 flew their Hellcats against Marcus Island for the Hellcat's combat debut.

The days spent flying out of Oceana paid off, as VF-9 acquitted itself well in combat, scoring 129 air-to-air victories before being ordered Stateside in March 1944. Many of the Oceana plankowners were aces. Lieutenant Junior Grade Eugene Valencia and Lieutenant Junior Grade Bill Bonneau each finished the deployment with seven victories. Valencia went on to score a total of twenty-three, ending up as the third-ranking Navy ace. Lieutenant Junior Grade Hamilton McWhorter was christened "One Slug" McWhorter for his deadly shooting that made him a double ace with VF-9 (he ended the war with a total of twelve). Lieutenant Mayo Hadden, Lieutenant Junior Grade Lou Menard and Lieutenant Junior Grade Marv Franger each downed eight aircraft.

Lieutenant Winters had to wait until June of 1944 to get "his" squadron into the Pacific war. Flying off *Lexington* he scored eight aerial victories and ended up as commander of Air Group 19—another Oceana plankowner who did well. VF-9 remained on the West Coast and did not return to Oceana. They split to form VF-12 and reformed at NAS Pasco, Washington, during the remainder of 1944 and were back at

View from inside the north tower at NAS Oceana. Right, a VF-21 FJ Fury taxis at the new south ramp with F7U Cutlasses in the background in the mid-1950s. *US Navy*

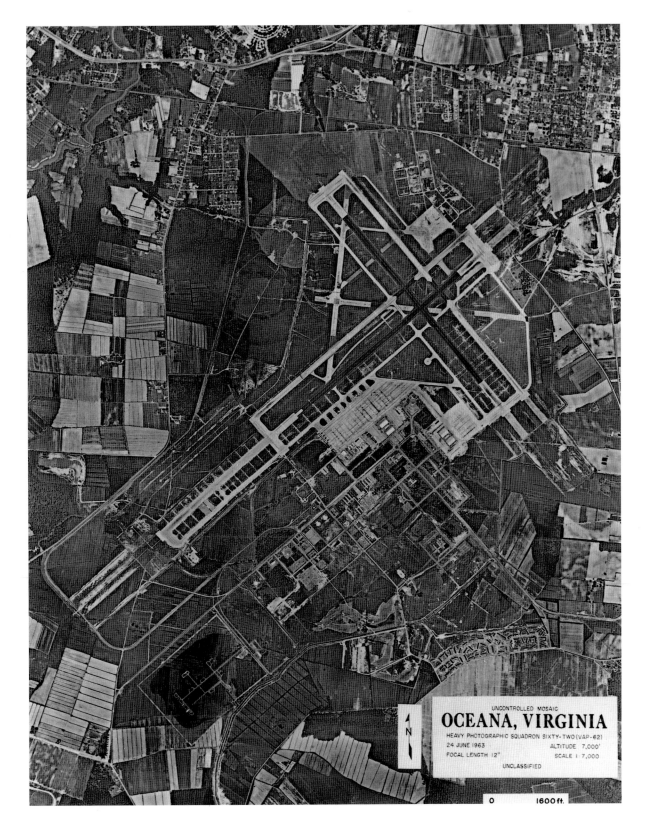

UNCONTROLLED MOSAIC

OCEANA, VIRGINIA

HEAVY PHOTOGRAPHIC SQUADRON SIXTY-TWO (VAP-62)

24 JUNE 1963   ALTITUDE 7,000'

FOCAL LENGTH 12"   SCALE 1:7,000

UNCLASSIFIED

N

0   1600 ft.

A 24 June 1963 aerial view of Oceana showing the new field and runways juxtaposed over the original field. *US Navy*

A division of A4D Skyhawks overfly the second "Miramar" hangar complex constructed at Oceana. At the time, Oceana was home to several carrier air groups. The aircraft of two air groups can be seen arrayed on the ramp in front of the hangar. Below, an aerial perspective of the south side. The twin curved roofs of the first "Miramar" hangar complex can be seen at the north end of the ramp. *US Navy*

sea by February of 1945, aboard USS *Lexington* this time.

Bigger and Better

After the departure of VF-9, upgrading of Oceana began in earnest. On August 17, 1943, Lieutenant Jesse Harley was installed as officer-in-charge and the Oceana field was officially commissioned as a naval auxiliary air station. Harley was to oversee an expansion that included accommodations for as many as 160 officers and 800 enlisted personnel (roughly three squadrons of a typical air group) and improving the runways to 6,000 feet of concrete. The field shut down to expedite construction, which progressed by the end of the year enough to allow Carrier Air Group 13 to move in on January 16, 1944. Building programs continued in order to keep pace with the numbers of aircraft and personnel practically pouring into the station. Commander F. E. Deam arrived on March 9, 1944, and was installed as the first commanding officer. Oceana continued to grow. By 1945, eight squadrons were operating out of Oceana.

At war's end many fields fell into disuse with the cutback in operating forces. Oceana, however, had proven its worth and was viewed as a valuable location because of its close proximity to the Norfolk complex. Two large air groups were stationed at the field along with a fleet aircraft service unit. The field continued to be busy right up the advent of the Korean conflict. The introduction of jet aircraft into front-line service resulted in Oceana being closed in September of 1950 to allow for lengthening of the runways another 2,000 feet. The field was chosen to play a central role in the transition of naval aviation from piston power to jet power.

Naval Air Station Oceana

On April 1, 1952, Oceana became a full-fledged naval air station. The station saw more and more jet traffic and in July, put its own auxiliary field, Naval Air Landing Facility Fentress, into operation. Fentress was specifically developed for field carrier landing practice. Its close proximity to Oceana allowed easy access for aircraft and landing signal officers with minimal transit time and kept the Oceana traffic pattern clear.

Oceana was designated an "all weather" air station in February 1954 and the big move to the southside began. The administration building was finished and occupied in June, followed by operations in July. The first of two large "Miramar" hangars (Hangar 200) was completed in that year, the second in 1957. The station continued to add structures on the southern side of the runways. Up to this point, a single large hangar was used on the "northside." Eight 372-man barracks were built along with the mark of any truly varsity naval air station: a commissary.

Master Jet Base

The field was given the name Apollo Soucek on June 4, 1957, and designated a "master jet base" in a gala ceremony that featured an open house and an airshow by the Blue Angels. Oceana was selected to play a major role in the massive base-loading plan in which similar aircraft would be co-located at master jet bases for maintenance ease and economy. Over the next few years, squadrons changed their homebases in concert with the plan. In 1959, VF-102 brought their F4D Skyrays to Oceana in preparation for eventual transition to the F4H Phantom, which had yet to arrive. Oceana was to be the home of the F4H (F-4) Phantom and the A2F (A-6) Intruder.

From 1949 to 1961, the Navy introduced no fewer than thirteen major types of fighter and attack aircraft. This caused severe problems because of continual transition training, com-

plex logistical support, and unacceptable accident rates. Among other changes to fix these problems, two new carrier replacement air groups (RCVGs or RAGs) were formed in 1958. The composition of these groups was primarily fleet squadrons that were given a change in mission. RCVG 12 was based on the West Coast to support the Pacific fleet squadrons and RCVG 4 was based on the East Coast, supporting the Atlantic fleet squadrons. Carrier Replacement Air Group 4 was made up of VF-101, VF-174, VA-42, and VA-44. These squadrons

A-4L Skyhawks on the Oceana ramp in the early 1970s. *US Navy*

are still referred to as RAGs even though their current official title is fleet readiness squadron (FRS).

The individual RAGs were spread out among the East Coast naval air stations and co-located with the fleet squadrons they supported. VF-101, VA-42, and VF-21 were to support Oceana-based aircraft. VF-101, a fleet F4D Skyray squadron, merged with the fleet all-weather training unit based in Key West. As a RAG it was equipped with F4D Skyrays and F3H Demons to train pilots for those aircraft and had F3D Skyknights, T-33B Shooting Stars, and R4D Skytrains for support. VF-101 was scheduled to add the F4H to its stable and established a VF-101 Detachment A at Oceana for F4H training. Eventually, the entire squadron moved to Oceana. VA-42 was a fleet AD

Skyraider squadron that moved into the RAG business. VF-21, previously a record-breaking fleet F9F-8 squadron that won the Battle "E" (award for squadron battle efficiency) for 1953, retained their current F11F Tigers and picked up F9F-8T Cougars, T-33B Shooting Stars, and T-28B Trojans. In November, the squadron relinquished the F11Fs for A4D Skyhawks and was redesignated VA-43 in July 1959.

The Phantom Arrives

(*Note*: Under the Military Aircraft Redesignation effective September 1, 1962, the Navy adopted an aircraft designation system in concert with the Air Force. For example, the F4H-1F became the F-4A Phantom and the A2F-1 became the A-6A Intruder. The authors have used designations as they applied during the time frames referred to in the text.)

The first VF-101 F4H-1F Phantom touched down on April 26, 1961, piloted by Commander

An aerial view of Oceana as it appeared in the late 1980s. The base is now in the center of ever-expanding Virginia Beach and no longer a lone outpost in the swampy wastelands. *US Navy.* Far left above, VF-171 F-4N Phantoms heading north along coastline returning to NAS Oceana. *US Navy.* Far left below, VF-171 F-4N Phantom taxis on the flight deck during carrier qualification. *US Navy.* Left, A Tactical Air Reconnaissance Pod System (TARPS) equipped Tomcat enters the break at Oceana. *Dave Parsons*

Gerald G. O'Rourke. VF-74 began transitioning to the Phantom in July, followed by VF-102 in December. Both squadrons deployed to the Mediterranean with their Phantoms within a year. The arrival of the Phantom marked a turning point in continuity of tactical aircraft. Unlike the relatively short life of aircraft introduced during the 1950s, the Phantom would stay at Oceana for more than twenty years. The A-6A Intruder arrived on February 1, 1963, to join VA-42, the designated Intruder RAG. (After almost thirty years of tenure at Oceana, there's still no end in sight.) The field increased in size from the original 328.5 acres to 8,000 acres.

"Fighter Country" was now on its way to being established. By the end of 1963, VF-74, VF-102, VF-14, and VF-41 were all flying the F-4B Phantom out of Oceana alongside VF-101 Detachment A. At the time, F-4s were teamed with F-8 Crusaders on the big-deck carriers. For the most part, Carrier Air Wings (CVW) included two fighter squadrons. Continuing the concept established in the 1950s, one squadron performed the all-weather interception mission and the other had the day-fighter role. This led to specifically developed aircraft. The remaining *Essex*-class carriers could not accommodate the Phantom and flew either two F-8 squadrons or an F-8 unit alongside an F-3B Demon squadron. The F-8 Crusader was the latest in day-fighter designs and had replaced the F11F Tiger and FJ-3 Fury. The heavier and larger radar-equipped Phantom replaced the

The NAS Oceana tower seen over the nose of a freshly painted low-visibility Tomcat, hence the absence of a dull finish and characteristic splotches of corrosion spot painting. *Dave Parsons.* Far left lower, the main gate sign at NAS Oceana simply states its mission: Master jet base for the Tomcat and Intruder. *Joe Leo.* Far left, an aerial view of the world's largest collection of Tomcats. The fighter ramp at Oceana, seen here in 1989, was at the time home to thirteen Tomcat squadrons. *Dave Parsons*

21

The Gypsy line. VF-32 Tomcats await aircrews with their canopies up. The first two are resplendent in their air-show markings. Fighter Wing 1 allows each squadron to paint two of their aircraft in the traditional colorful Navy markings. *Garry English.* Far right, VF-101 Grim Reaper maintenance personnel conduct the vital troubleshooting and repair. *Joe Leo*

F3H Demon and F4D Skyray in the all-weather interceptor role. Both missions eventually would be merged and performed by the Phantom.

In 1963, the Phantom was still being worked into the interceptor mission and its air-to-air prowess yet to be discovered. The Demon's days were numbered and the last East Coast-based Demon squadron to make a cruise returned in May of 1964. Shortly thereafter, either the Phantom or Crusader replaced all Demons in Navy squadrons.

As the A-4 was replaced by the A-7 Corsair, VA-43 dropped its A-4 RAG responsibilities and took on instrument refresher training as a

so-called instrument RAG. As part of the revamping of the fighter training program in 1969, VA-43 took on adversary duties as well with its TA-4Js. The aftermath of the Ault report, the Navy's introspective look at the way air-to-air training was conducted (brought on by less than optimum results in Vietnam), led to the advent of the Navy Fighter Weapons School (Topgun) at NAS Miramar and widespread emphasis on dissimilar air combat training. Subsequent success during renewed air-to-air combat over North Vietnam in 1972-73 brought even more emphasis on dissimilar air combat training. This also brought about a change in paint scheme for some of

VA-43's aircraft to camouflage patterns reflecting threat aircraft. The squadron eventually took on more adversary work than instrument training and changed its designation to VF-43.

Enter the Tomcat

The F-14 Tomcat was the next aircraft to become a resident of Fighter Country. The Tomcat made its maiden flight at the Grumman factory in December 1970. Fleet introduction came in October 1972 at NAS Miramar with VF-1 and VF-2. Oceana got its first Tomcats in 1974 when VF-14 and VF-32 traded in their F-4 Phantoms. In 1976, VF-101 stood up as the East Coast F-14 fleet readiness squadron and turned over responsibility for F-4 training to VF-171. Over the next few years, VF-84 and VF-41 transitioned while VF-142 and VF-143 came east from Miramar to become Oceana Tomcat squadrons. VF-11 and VF-31 traded in their F-4 Phantoms for Tomcats during 1980. In 1981, VF-33 and VF-102 returned from an extended Indian Ocean cruise and turned in their aging F-4J Phantoms. In January 1982, they received their first Tomcats. Oceana became an all-Tomcat fighter wing when the last two F-4 squadrons, VF-74 and VF-103, began their transition in 1983. VF-171 continued to train F-4 crews for NAS Miramar- and USS *Midway*-based squadrons until 1987 when it was disestablished.

Smile, Baby

Oceana Tomcats received a new mission in 1981 when the Tactical Air Reconnaissance Pod System (TARPS) arrived. The TARPS pod was the answer to the impending departure of dedicated photo reconnaissance aircraft (RA-5 and RF-8) from the fleet. Rather than develop an aircraft solely for the purpose of photo reconnaissance, the Naval Air Development Center produced a pod capable of carrying three sensors. Each carrier air wing had one of its F-14 squadrons designated for the TARPS role. The TARPS squadron received three pods, three F-14s modified to carry the pod, additional maintenance personnel for care and maintenance of the pod, and intelligence specialists to evaluate the film.

Oceana's Resident Bandits

Meanwhile the VF-43 Challengers continued to improve their support to the Oceana

VF-14 Tophatter Tomcats show off their seventieth-anniversary markings on their two showbirds. VF-14 is the oldest and longest continuously active squadron in the Navy. *Joe Leo*

combat with missiles and guns. Missiles can be "fired" and the system calculates whether it is a "kill" or a miss. Best of all, the system records the entire engagement so it can be played back later. Aircrews are exposed to the latest threat simulations of aircraft and tactics during FFARP. Through the latter 1970s and early 1980s, VF-43 used a mix of A-4 and F-5 aircraft for threat simulations. In 1985, the F-5s were replaced with Israeli Kfir C1 aircraft (US designation F-23). These were used until April 1988. The squadron began using F-16N Falcons in 1989, and F-5s returned in 1990 alongside the venerable and still very viable A-4s.

US Navy 2, Libya 0

Oceana-based Tomcats captured world attention in August 1981 when Libyan Su-22 Fitters fired upon two VF-41 Tomcats. The Tomcats evaded the missile and engaged the Fitters. Each Tomcat maneuvered behind a Fitter and downed it with an AIM-9 Sidewinder. In 1983, Tomcats were called upon to exercise their TARPS skill in combat operations over Grenada and Lebanon. VF-32 saw action in both areas. VF-31 and VF-143 both were on the cutting edge over Lebanon in which they flew highly vulnerable photo recon missions over hostile areas.

You Can Run, But You Can't Hide

In an unprecedented and highly dramatic operation in October 1985, four Tomcats from the USS *Saratoga* made a night interception of an Egyptian airliner carrying terrorist hijackers from the *Achille Lauro* tragedy and forced it to land in Italy where police arrested the terrorists. For VF-74 and VF-103, it was a mission not far removed from the Tomcat's normal trade: aircraft interception and escort. Again, Tomcats made front-page news.

Oceana Tomcats were in the thick of international news in March 1986 when Libya established a so-called Line of Death in the Gulf of Sidra. During three carrier battle group maneuvers in the gulf to protest Libya's false extension of its territorial waters, Libya fired SA-5 missiles at two VF-102 Tomcats that were over international waters. When patrol boats ventured towards the carriers that night, they were fired upon and sunk. Tomcats provided around-the-clock combat air patrol (CAP)

Tomcat squadrons by developing the Fleet Fighter Air Combat Maneuvering Readiness Program (FFARP), which is incorporated into each squadron's turnaround training cycle. During FFARP, an entire squadron goes through an air combat maneuvering syllabus, working up from one-versus-one to multi-section engagements, all of which are monitored and recorded on the Tactical Aircrew Combat Training System. This system uses instruments and sensors on the aircraft and on the ground that allow realistic simulation of air

Approaching the hangar area from the road, there is no doubt where you are: Fighter Country! Below, in late 1991, the first Tomcat gate guard was put into place. VF-143, the winners of the Battle "E" that year, proudly adorned the early block Tomcat with their markings. *Joe Leo*

Two views of the cavernous hangar bays of Hangar 404, one of three fighter hangars at Oceana. Here, maintenance taking several days is usually performed. Routine jobs are undertaken on the flight line. Navy maintenance troops are the world's best at rapid repair in the most arduous conditions. Far right, a VF-101 Grim Reaper maintenance trooper works on the tail of a Tomcat. As a shore-based squadron, VF-101 has over 1,000 personnel including many women. *Joe Leo*

which the Libyans wisely chose not to challenge with their aircraft. Perhaps they recalled the events in August 1981.

After a Libyan-sponsored terrorist bombing of a nightclub in Germany that was frequented by American servicemen, two carrier battle groups still in the Mediterranean Sea launched strikes against Libya in concert with Air Force F-111Fs flying out of England. Oceana-based Tomcats from VF-33 and VF-102 flying off the USS *America* flew cover for A-6 Intruders from USS *America* and USS *Coral Sea* and for the Air Force F-111s. No Libyan aircraft challenged the Tomcats.

US Navy 4, Libya 0

Libyan aircraft did not challenge Tomcats until January 1989 when two Libyan MiG-23 Floggers were detected heading towards the USS *Kennedy*. VF-32 Tomcats were vectored to intercept. After the two aircraft did not turn away and exhibited hostile intent, the F-14s took the Floggers under fire. Missiles downed both Floggers with no damage to the F-14s.

Oceana today encompasses more than 5,000 acres of land. No longer a wasteland or isolated base far from civilization, the base is hemmed in on all sides with housing, shopping malls, and industrial parks. Instead of a wooden tower with unreliable radios and barely enough runway for an F4F Wildcat, the base has more than seven miles of runway that routinely land everything in the US inventory up to and including the gigantic C-5A Galaxy. The field averages as many as 11,000 takeoffs and landings per month—one every two minutes. Its air-traffic control facility controls 94,000 square miles of airspace. The latest count shows twenty-four squadrons at Oceana. Of these, ten are fleet F-14 squadrons, one is the F-14 replacement squadron, and two are in the adversary business. These Tomcat squadrons make Oceana Fighter Country.

Hangar 404-1, home to the VF-101 Grim Reapers and as the sign indicates, Tomcat Alley. *Dave Parsons.* Right, ordnancemen haul a Sidewinder cart back to the hangar after mounting a practice Sidewinder on a Tomcat. Protective headgear that includes ear and eye protection must be worn at all times on the flight line. *Joe Leo*

Proud squadron insignia are seen all around Oceana. Here, one of the VF-31 Tomcatter showbirds taxis on the ramp. *Dave Parsons.* Below, the VF-84 Jolly Rogers insignia adorns the wall of Hangar 404-1. *Dave Parsons.* Below left, the VF-14 Tophatters insignia on another wall. *Joe Leo*

A VF-32 Tomcat just after takeoff from NAS Roosevelt Roads, Puerto Rico, during a detachment. *Dave Parsons.* Right, NTU means NAS Oceana in FAA parlance. The lighted sign is positioned at the hold-short area of the runway and allows aircrews to check the performance of their TACAN, the primary navigation aid, prior to takeoff. In the background, a VF-32 Swordsmen Tomcat awaits takeoff clearance. *Garry English.* Far right, Two VF-14 Tomcats in contrasting paint schemes fly in formation over the Atlantic Ocean near Puerto Rico during USS *John F. Kennedy*'s stop-and-go workups in 1989-90. *Dave Parsons*

NTU TACAN - CH 113
BRG-257
DIST-0.9 MI.

Chapter 2

A Year in the Life of a Tomcat Squadron

The RAG

Before reporting to a fleet squadron, each aircrew goes through the RAG. Originally known as a Replacement Air Group, its formal designation is now Fleet Readiness Squadron (FRS). Both terms, however, are used interchangeably on an informal basis.

The RAG is much larger than a fleet F-14 squadron. VF-101, the Grim Reapers, supports ten fleet squadrons based at Oceana and has three times as many aircraft and four times as many personnel as a fleet squadron. The RAG is a crossroads for the fighter community. Aircrews constantly cycle through the training syllabus en route to the fleet. At the same time, aircrews return from the fleet after several years to become instructors. The RAG performs a vital role in training aircrews for all the fleet squadrons in Fighter Wing 1. As a result, it becomes a melting pot for tactics and standardization for the squadrons it serves.

At the RAG, replacement aircrew are elevated above their previous status as aviators without wings in the training command, but find themselves still under constant scrutiny and grading. The term "replacement" is used rather than student, although many instructors call them "studs" (short for student) or "cones" (short for coneheads). Newly winged pilots and radar intercept officers (RIOs) are Category (Cat) 1 replacements. Aircrew with previous time in the F-14 or other aircraft are given other designations—Cat 2, 3, or 4 depending on the amount of refresher or transition training needed. Cat 1 replacements get the full syllabus, which lasts roughly a year depending on a variety of influencing factors, including aircraft availability, the replacement's progress, and importantly, the weather.

The Officer's Club

When a Cat 1 completes the syllabus and becomes "ready for issue" to the fleet, he becomes a "nugget." Although the RAG exposes the Cat 1 aircrew to the various skills needed to master the fighter mission, the squadron provides some needed final polishing when the nugget checks onboard. The Cat 1 replacements also find that not all their training takes place in the formal classroom or cockpit. Informal training takes place at the Oceana Officer's Club. Though not required, virtually every replacement finds himself at happy hour or the standing-room-only Wednesday and Friday nights at the club. At the "O" club (or just plain "club"), replacements are exposed to "hangar flying" and the game of dice. Over the varnished wood of the bar, the lore of the fighter community is told—the great exploits and the not-so-great, the legendary characters (such as Joe "Hoser" Satrapa) and their colorful tales. Here they learn, as in any close-knit, select community, the social pecking order and the unwritten standards by which all members are judged.

Virtually no gathering at the club passes without bringing out the dice cup. The game is formally known as "horse and hammer," but it is universally referred to as "dice" or to "bring out the dice." A leather cup that holds five die is

The well-known Tomcat patch. Left, the Tomcat's mission doesn't end when the sun goes down. Squadrons must devote a healthy percentage of their flying to night missions to be able to defend the battle group around the clock. *Dave Parsons*

The main entrance to VF-101 is graced by this canopy. VF-101, the East Coast replacement air group (RAG), is four times as large as a typical fleet squadron having over 1,000 officer and enlisted staff instructor, maintenance, administrative, and support personnel, as well as the average load of aircrews and maintenance troops under instruction. *Joe Leo.* Below, VF-101's flightline includes both F-14A and A Plus Tomcats as the RAG trains aircrews and maintenance personnel for assignment to both. Only VF-101 is assigned the F-14A Plus (now called F-14B) and trains personnel for the four Oceana and two Miramar F-14A Plus squadrons. *Dave Parsons*

34

A lineup of VF-101 Tomcats caught during an unusually quiet moment. It is far more typical to see gaps in the line because so many sorties are being flown. A typical day at VF-101 begins with flights at daybreak and continues far into the night, especially during field carrier landing practice (FCLP), which entails multiple night sorties to prepare for carrier qualification (CQ). Maintenance personnel work around the clock to provide a steady supply of "up" Tomcats to feed the flight schedule. *Joe Leo.* Below, a Tomcat aircrew's office. Despite an initial impression of being crammed with knobs, switches, instruments, displays, and pushbuttons, the cockpit is quite roomy relative to other fighter aircraft. *Craig Dugan*

a common feature at all Navy and Marine officer's clubs and is alternately rolled by all participants. After each round of rolling, the highest combination is out (for example, five sixes wins over five fives); the first out must order a round for the group and ensure it arrives before the last player is out or he must buy another round. If a die falls off the playing surface or the cup is rolled short a die, a round is owed. Players are eliminated until the last two go head-to-head in a best-of-three series that takes a little luck and a sound knowledge of dice tactics to win. Replacements usually end up buying a healthy percentage of rounds until they acquire a feel for the game's strategy.

At the club, the replacements also meet the members of the fleet squadrons they are working so hard to join. Though not unlike a fraternity rush, gatherings at the club let the fleet squadrons in need of replacement aircrew check out the "talent" in the RAG, while the replacements gain information on which squadrons they'd like to join. The final selection will involve a variety of factors based on the individ-

ual's choice, the squadron priority (based on phase of training or deployment), and grade-point average. The result is similar to professional sports college draft picks as top talent is spread between the twelve fleet squadrons to ensure no squadron gets a disproportionate number of stars, and vice versa.

At the club and in the squadron, replacements learn the lingo and dress code of the fighter community. If a replacement has seen the movie *Top Gun* too many times and adorns his flight jacket with extraneous patches, it is not long before the instructors make a "suggestion" to adhere to the time-honored tradition of wearing only those patches that have been earned. Patches are a rite of passage and at this point a Cat 1 can wear the Tomcat patches and a nametag, but usually little else. It is definitely not cool for a replacement to wear a squadron patch or base patch from the training base at Pensacola. The safest bet is to wear a "virgin" leather jacket and wait until the pilot has accumulated enough patches (typically, the end of the first cruise). On the other hand, the

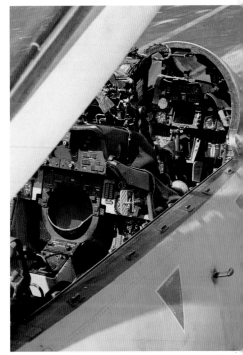

flight jackets of the instructors are veritable mosaics of various patches that serve as visual biographies of the wearer's career. A quick glance at the jacket reveals the fleet squadron(s) the instructor has served in, type and dates of cruises, number of traps, special achievements such as landing signal officer, missile firings, Top Ten landing proficiency, and combat (Gulf of Sidra Yacht Club, Desert Shield, or Desert Storm), and competitions participated in like Reconnaissance Air Meets or Grand Slam. The wearing of these patches is considered a holy rite of passage not to be rushed.

The Hit Board

Transgressions of accepted behavior such as wearing inappropriate patches, guffaws, or even communication mistakes heard over the radio are duly inscribed on a "hit board" prominently displayed in the ready room. The hit board lists the transgression, the hitter (person making the accusation), and the hittee (person accused of the transgression). Everyone from the CO down to the junior member of the command is fair game for the hit board, although it would be a rare occasion for someone to hit the CO. It is typical, however, to see the junior members of the command on the hit board quite frequently, especially the Cat 1 replacements. The hittee is free to counter-hit his accuser, which often leads to a string of counter-hits, but the Cat 1 replacements

The pilot's office as it appears at 21,000 feet on a combat air patrol mission. The greenish display in the center is the vertical display indicator (VDI), which is the primary aircraft attitude indicator. Below it is another cathode ray tube (CRT), which is the Horizontal Situation Display that gives the pilot a repeat of what the RIO's tactical information display (TID) is. *Craig Dugan.* Right, a Tomcat aircrew during preflight of a VF-101 Tomcat. *Joe Leo.* Far right, one of the preflight checklist items is the engine bay. The plane captain will have the "daily" door (the curved door seen here, which is the most frequently opened door where routine servicing is accomplished after each flight as opposed to the larger "weekly" door to the left which is not opened as often) unlatched to ease inspection by the aircrew. *Joe Leo*

36

quickly learn that it is not advisable to take on instructors who are fleet veterans with years of hit-board experience under their belts. In general, hits are done with an air of humor, but still carry a subtle message of conformity. When enough hits are accumulated, a kangaroo court is held and the ready room membership rules on each hit after the hitter and hittee present their case. Excuses are not tolerated and will result in a stiffer fine than the $1.00 per hit standard fine. For most, the board is a daily source of entertainment and for a few who seem to be popular and frequent hittees, it can be a source of pain and embarrassment. It is probably the most often read board in the ready room along with the flight schedule.

The Classroom

Initially, the replacements spend weeks in classrooms, working with self-study computers and simulators before their first flight in the Tomcat. Once the flights begin, lectures, computer work, and simulators continue through each phase of the RAG syllabus.

Familiarization or FAM is the first phase in which the aircrews learn the basic operation, emergency procedures, and flight characteristics of the Tomcat.

Basic Fleet Air Superiority (BFAS) is next where instructors teach basic employment of the Tomcat as an aerial weapons system. In this phase, the aircrews learn about the weapons carried by the Tomcat and how to use them in tactical situations. By the end of BFAS, the aircrews are proficient at running intercepts at various altitudes and airspeeds. As the aircrews gain experience, they move closer to the difficult challenges of the final phases of the RAG syllabus: aerial gunnery, tactics, carrier qualification, and advanced fleet air superiority. It is in these phases that some aircrews wash out.

Air Combat Maneuvering

An all-important part of the training syllabus is air combat maneuvering, called the "tactics" phase at VF-101. Air combat maneuvering poses stringent requirements for weather, which is not always satisfactory year-round at Oceana, especially during the winter. Classes routinely deploy as a whole to NAS Key West, Florida, to take advantage of the year-round superb weather and uncontested airspace. VF-101 has permanent spaces at Key

Although the pilot has control of the aircraft in the air, on the flight line, the plane captain directs the pilot's actions from engine start through preflight checks and until he gives taxi commands out of the line. Standardized hand signals are used by the plane captain and aircrew to allow rapid communication. For troubleshooting problems, maintenance personnel can plug into the aircraft with a headset and talk to the aircrew directly. *Joe Leo.* Below, the firing port of the six-barreled Vulcan cannon is made of titanium to withstand the high temperatures generated when the cannon fires at the rate of 3,000 20mm rounds per minute. *Dave Parsons*

When the Tomcat returns to the line, a plane captain is waiting to direct the aircraft into place. Here, a plane captain uses hand signals to turn the Tomcat toward its parking spot where another plane captain is waiting with further directions. Once parked, he will direct the pilot through the shutdown sequence and receive, along with maintenance troubleshooters, a quick debriefing on the condition of the aircraft. *Joe Leo.* Right, the power of the 30,000 pounds of thrust (each) of the F110 engines that make this an F-14A Plus Tomcat is evident in this view of a Tomcat in full "blower." *Bruce Trombecky*

West co-located with VF-45, whose A-4s and F-16s are routinely used as adversaries.

Proficiency in the tactics phase marks the "blooding" of a fighter aircrew. Keeping sight of all participants in a multi-bogey engagement, flying the Tomcat to the edge of its performance envelope, and employing its weapons before someone else employs one against you are distinct challenges. Gaining situational awareness in this fast-moving, high-G arena that can span miles of sky is difficult. Losing it is easy. Difficulty in mastering the art of air combat maneuvering stems from the challenge of having to take in the visual and verbal inputs, assess the spatial relationships, and make split-second decisions in constantly changing fight that ranges from zero to supersonic speeds across the sky, against experienced adversaries.

Carrier Qualification

The carrier qualification phase is equally challenging and can be the largest hurdle to successfully completing the RAG syllabus. Naval aviators fresh out of the training command already have passed the test of a carrier aviator by landing the T-2 and TA-4 aboard a carrier. However, aviators must pass again in the Tomcat *and*, for the first time, at night.

The F-14 is not the easiest nor the prettiest aircraft to bring aboard a carrier. Its ungainly looking approach configuration has earned it the affectionate name of "Turkey." Cat 1 RIOs will go to the boat in the backseat of an instructor or higher category pilot and do not face the tremendous pressure that pilots endure in completing carrier qualification.

Before going to "the boat," all aircrew spend many nights at Fentress Field, ten miles south of Oceana, practicing carrier landings under the watchful and grading eyes of the landing signal officers. Fentress has a simulated carrier deck laid out complete with lighting that gives each aircrew the correct sight picture as they fly the pattern. Each pass is graded by the landing signal officer for later debrief and trend analysis. The aircrews will go to the boat only after seemingly endless field landing practice and the landing signal officer's determination that they are ready.

No amount of practice at Fentress can remove the heart-thumping feeling when the aircrew arrives over the boat awaiting their

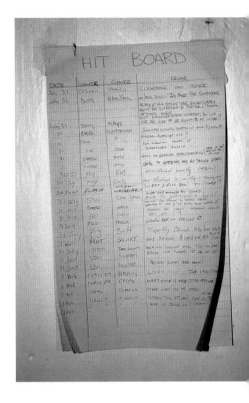

turn at the real thing, and the most satisfying words a pilot can hear over the radio after the prescribed number of day and night traps, typically spanning several days, is "you're a qual." Not all pilots qualify during the first attempt at carrier qualification and most are given another chance after repeating the endless practice at Fentress and waiting for another carrier qualification period.

"Ready for Issue"

The aircrews spend the better part of a year mastering the basics of flying the Tomcat, tactical employment in fleet air superiority and air combat maneuvering, carrier qualification, air-to-air gunnery, and low-level flying. Then the replacement aircrew is "ready for issue" to a fleet squadron. This is a long-awaited event since aircrews are anxious to stop being students and join their fleet squadron. Fledgling Tomcat crews, by this time, have probably earned a callsign, which is an early rite of passage that ranks with the earning of their wings and being issued a leather flight jacket. They have been immersed in fighter jargon for

Even a detachment to Key West, Florida, gives replacements no relief from the hit board. This impromptu hit board recorded the transgressions during a two week tactics detachment to NAS Key West. A kangaroo court held at the conclusion of the detachment generated cash at the rate of one dollar a hit (whining brings additional fines). *Dave Parsons.* Above left, one of the rites of passage that replacement aircrews look forward to is the painting of their name on the canopy rail of the Tomcat, which only occurs after they reach their fleet squadron. Although all squadron aircraft carry the name of an aircrew, no jets are actually assigned to individual crews. *Garry English*

39

This photo plainly illustrates the year-round advantage of NAS Key West's beautiful weather that is necessary for air combat maneuvering (ACM). VF-101 routinely detaches to Key West for the tactics and sometimes aerial gunnery phases of the RAG syllabus. Replacements can complete in two weeks what might take six weeks or longer at NAS Oceana due to weather, adversary availability, and competition for assets. *Dave Parsons.* Below, the F-4 Phantom gate guard sports the markings of VF-101 after a semi-permanent detachment status resulted in spaces dedicated to the Grim Reapers being established in 1989. Previously, the Phantom carried the markings of VF-171, the F-4 RAG that maintained a permanent ACM detachment at Key West for years before its disestablishment. *Dave Parsons.* Far right, a VF-103 Tomcat flies past NAS Key West. In the background are the pristine skies that make Key West so attractive for ACM training. *Dave Parsons*

VF-41 Tomcats climb in formation against the backdrop of the vast ranges at NAS Fallon, Nevada. Near the end of an air wing's turnaround training, it deploys as a whole to Fallon for strike planning and execution training, which includes intensive live-weapons practice. Prior to that, the nine squadrons comprising an air wing conduct individual training at their home fields, which are dispersed among five naval air stations across the country. *Bob Lawson.* Far left above, a VF-101 Tomcat and a VF-45 F-16N await takeoff clearance at NAS Key West prior to a tactics ACM flight. The F-16 simulates the latest fourth-generation threat aircraft and is a formidable, but not impossible challenge for the Tomcat. A replacement pilot has his hands full when taking on this aircraft, which has impressive thrust-to-weight, acceleration, and turning characteristics. *Dave Parsons.* Far left below, the VF-45 Blackbirds, an adversary squadron permanently based at NAS Key West, provide adversary services to VF-101 during tactics detachments. The squadron flies F-16N and A-4E/F aircraft in the adversary role primarily in support of the F/A-18 squadrons at NAS Cecil Field. The red stars and threat paint schemes leave no doubt as to their mission. *Dave Parsons*

A VF-43 Skyhawk returns to NAS Oceana after an ACM sortie. The subsonic but nimble Skyhawk is a valuable and low-cost tool in the adversary trade. *Bruce Trombecky.* Below, VF-43 operated the Israeli-built Kfir C1 from 1985 to 1988. *Ken Neubauer.* Far right below, a carrier is virtually a small city and can steam for long periods of time. Support ships such as this are configured to transfer fuel, weapons, food, and any other supplies the carrier needs including toilet paper. *US Navy.* Far right above, two VF-41 Tomcats race across the Nevada desert near Fallon. Fallon offers vast ranges and target complexes not available at Oceana. *Bob Lawson*

months now and can "talk" with their hands with reasonable proficiency.

Aircrew Callsigns

At some point during almost every aviator's career, a callsign gets attached to the aviator's usual name. Sometimes he or she will pick one up in the training command and it will stick for an aviator's entire career. Sometimes aviators collect several during their careers, trading them off as their reputation or demeanor changes.

The callsigns themselves are extremely diverse. They range from obvious to obscure, from cute to obscene, from clever to silly. What they share is an appropriateness that is not always easy to explain. They fit and they stick, at least for a while. Once they've stuck, you hear them around the ready room, and you see them on flight-jacket nametags and on squadron coffee mugs. A true callsign is one that, when you hear a guy's real first name (such as "Tom" or "Bill"), it sounds unfamiliar and odd.

Wives very rarely use callsigns to refer to their husbands. The prevailing spousal attitude is that callsigns are childish and represent a part of the husbands that they (the wives) would just as soon the husbands grow out of.

A few poor souls never get callsigns at all, although that is an unusual situation. It generally means that the person in question is either colorless or unpopular, or that he takes himself much too seriously. One F-14 backseater recalls two guys who, although their squadron mates

Commander Bob Davis of VF-32 converses with two maintenance personnel aboard USS *John F. Kennedy*. Tireless efforts under harsh working conditions by dedicated maintenance troops are necessary to keep the aircraft at a high state of readiness. *Dave Parsons*. Right, a typical after-hours scene in a junior officer (JO) bunkroom includes a friendly game of Nintendo or a book. No self-respecting bunkroom is without Nintendo, a sound and video system including a CD player, and a good library of videotapes. *Craig Dugan*. Above right, carriers are cruise ships and aren't known for their luxury accommodations. This typical JO bunkroom is shown during an impromptu gathering of VF-102 aircrews and ferry crews. *Pete Caulk*

tried repeatedly to give them callsigns, never seemed to get one that could stick.

There are a few basic rules that the assignment of callsigns seems to follow. You should never make one up for yourself, lest you run the risk of making it seem like you are trying to act cool. And squadrons should never make crash-program decisions such as "OK, everyone needs a callsign, where's the roster?" and proceed to dole out spur-of-the-moment monikers. Although there are strong philosophic connections, it isn't quite like in the cruise-classic movie *Animal House*, when the frat guys name the two new pledges "Pinto" and "Flounder."

Callsigns (and their close relatives, nicknames) reach well back into the annals of aviation. Circa 1930, now-famous aviators already sported nicknames such as "Squash," "Country," and "Stiffy." When Eugene Ely made the first trap aboard USS *Pennsylvania*, the ship's skipper was Charles "Frog" Pond. Theodore Ellyson was called "Spuds," a callsign later given to aviators who either had or came close to ramp strikes (near the "spud locker" on ancient aircraft carriers). The aviator for which Saufley Field would be named was called "Caswell." NAS Oceana was formally called Apollo Soucek airfield; Soucek's nickname was "Sockem."

The official "History of Airgroup 32" (compiled in 1944) also includes a list of "famous nicknames." Among those of VF-32: "Little Caesar" Outlaw (the skipper, who racked up six kills on the cruise); "Grey Fox" Preston; "Trigger" Merkel; "Hard Luck" Ladley; "J.A.P." Pond (short for John Alden Pond); "Spanky" McNair; "Plug" Terrill; and "Sleepy" Slocomb. One of the nicknames was the familiar, humorous variant on the sound of a pilot's last name: "Budapest" Hudspeth. Two members picked up a pair of nicknames each: "Cotton" Steinreide (also "Hoog"), and "Duck Belly" Palmer (also "Silent Sam"). And one of the nicknames ranks among the more mysterious and unusual—"Depopolus Benito" Meardon.

Aerial view of USS *America* taken by a VF-102 TARPS Tomcat. The landing area is clear in readiness for returning aircraft. The E-2 on the bow catapult is moments from launching. *US Navy.* Left, as a pilot comes aboard, he is working hard to be on glidescope (height), on centerline, and on speed. *US Navy*

VF-32's nicknames included "Broadway" Jones, "Scoop Jr." Dooley (also "Shadow"), "Stud" Stirling, and "Big Stoop" Armstrong. The history also points out that "Clem" Street was "protestingly known as 'Huey' and characteristically called 'Ant eater' by his hecklers." The reference to hecklers makes the point that, as far back as World War II, nicknames weren't always complimentary, and sometimes had an element of teasing.

The history also lists the names of the ten officers killed during training and combat. The list includes the nicknames "Monk" and "Dagwood."

A history of VF-3 from 1943 to 1945 also includes plenty of World War II nicknames: "Pup" Jones, "Pee Wee" Spalding, "Bashful" Burton, "Jetter" Lindsey (who also collected the handles "Pack Rat" and "Small Stores"), "Swampy" Creel, "Maidenswoon" English, "Rider" Moore, "Ghoulish" Gourley, and "Pinocchio" Thienes. Two squadron members— "Speedy" Bacchus and "Yellowhand" Tyler— showed up late aboard USS *Essex* after the squadron's final fling in San Francisco, "with a pair of wild tales that might have appeared within the covers of *True Confessions* magazine," the history said.

Glancing back at aviation history, it seems as if almost everything associated with flying got a nickname. Certainly the aircraft did— "Fury," "Hellcat," and so on. Aircraft carriers also received less-formal handles: The original USS *Lexington* (CV-3) was called "Lady Lex," but the second *Lexington* (CV-16) was nicknamed the "Blue Ghost." USS *Intrepid*, after being bombed and torpedoed, was sometimes referred to as the "Decrepit." Among today's carriers, the USS *John F. Kennedy* is called "Big John"; USS *Forrestal* is called "Forest Fire"; and USS *Abraham Lincoln* is simply referred to as "Abe."

These days, if you read through the squadron public affairs office releases in the back of *The Hook*, you'll find plenty of callsigns that are easy to understand given the popular frames of reference for aviators: "Oprah" Winfrey and Phil "Fess" Parker (television), "Omar" Bradley and Wright "Wilbur" McLeod (aviation history), Bobbie "Janis" McGee and "Tina" Turner (rock music). Most callsigns derive from last names, although the list above includes an unusual first-name derivative.

Perhaps the easiest genre of callsigns involves simple plays on the sound of names: "Snatch" Snachko, "Voodoo" Voors, "Boner" Bornarth, "Cracker" McCracken, "Stash" Fristachi. Others are based on puns or cliches: "Peachy" Keene, "Ice" Berg, and "Rock" Pyle.

Not all callsigns are particularly complimentary: "Sewer," "Wimpy," "Bhagwan," "Noid," "Ratbreath," and "Puke" come to mind. An aviator usually picks up the latter callsign by blowing lunch in an aircraft or at a squadron party. Even though callsigns like these don't sound cool, aviators get subtle points for living with them and not complaining.

Other callsigns are catchalls. Some Orientals are called "Fuji," guys with Polish names are called "Ski." A rare aviator gets christened with a custom-made, perfect callsign, such as Wilk O. West—"Wilco."

Many of the best callsigns come from specific habits or events in an aviator's life; to understand the origin of the name, you have to have known the aviator for a while. Douglas "Wrong Way" Corrigan is the classic example of this trend. Someone with the callsign "Boomer" is either a party hound or else broke

An EA-3 Skywarrior flanked by two A-7 Corsairs overflies USS *America*. *US Navy*. Left, an alert crew stands ready to launch. *Dave Parsons*. Far left above, a night launch of an F/A-18 Hornet. *PH2 Didas*. Far left below, USS *America* surrounded by its battle group heads across the Atlantic Ocean in February 1986 to join USS *Saratoga* and USS *Coral Sea* off the coast of Libya. In March, all three carriers engaged in combat with Libyan patrol boats and surface-to-air missile batteries, followed by strikes against Libya in April. *US Navy*

some windows with a supersonic low-level fly-by. "Sheets" probably spends a lot of time in the rack. "Beads" is sweating the load all the time, worrying about stuff. Stay around for forty years and chalk up 22,600 hours, as did Patrick Byrne, and folks will probably start calling you "Pappy," too.

Here's an off-the-cuff sampling from the former squadron buds of Lieutenant Ward Carroll, an F-14 radar intercept officer and former editor of *Approach* magazine: "Rex" (because he went on a crash diet and started looking anorexic); "Harpo" (he had a curly mop of hair); "Munster" (from his first name, Herman); "Tapeworm" (because he was skinny, and also made the mistake of telling everyone that he hated the callsign, which is a kiss of death if you really want to get rid of it). Carroll himself, at six feet four inches, picked up the obvious callsign "Stork" early in his career, and later "Mooch" (for always "borrowing" stamps, pens, paper clips, sodas, dollars, and so on).

Lieutenant Commander Dave Parsons, co-author of this book and also a former editor of the Naval Safety Center's *Approach* magazine, earned the callsign "Hey Joe" during one cruise: it is a slang term for the native vendors

that appear on the piers and on street corners in foreign ports, hawking souvenirs with the line "Hey Joe, special deal for you." Parsons garnered the nickname for his success in designing and selling T-shirts and posters.

Many callsigns are obscure to non-aviators, and require elaborate explanations, Commander John "Pogo" Reid's nickname, for example. To "pogo" during airborne radio communications means to switch to another channel, then quickly back to the original one. Early in his flying career, Reid mistook this instruction for someone else's callsign during an airborne radio transmission, answering, "Uh, roger, Pogo . . . ." The nickname, he recalls, was immediate, as soon as the story made the rounds of the squadron after they landed.

The genesis of callsigns is vividly and accurately described in the following passages from an unpublished novel, "A Glass Broken" by Lieutenant Ward Carroll.

As the novel opens, one of the two protagonists has just been roused from a nap he had been taking in the ready room. He is on cruise with the squadron aboard the boat.

Lieutenant Ted "Punk" Stephens slowly lifted his frame out of the chair and imme-diately felt the price for dozing in the sitting position. He winced and bent over to stretch out his lower back. He glanced at his watch. 0355.

Punk and his radar intercept officer, Lieutenant Commander Frank "Spud" Riley, grabbed their helmets and nav bags and made their way along the passageway. Spud had earned his callsign the hard way: two ejections and a ramp strike that fortunately resulted in an arrested landing. "Spud" was short for "spud locker," which was slang for the area just below the flight deck at the back of the carrier.

Stephens and Riley go out on the darkened deck to relieve another aircrew in the alert jet.

"Hey, pal! Time for the first team to come in," Ted yelled to the pilot seated in the F-14. The pilot, Lieutenant Dave "Biff" McDonald, directed his flashlight from the paperback he had been reading directly into Ted's eyes.

"Christ, Biff. So much for seeing at night."

"Sorry, Punk. I didn't know it was you. I heard this voice and got real scared."

Ted had earned the callsign "Punk" one day in the eight-man stateroom that was typical of the spaces junior officers called home during

A Royal Air Force F-4 Phantom escorts a Bear D north of the British Isles. This photo was taken by an F-14 that had been escorting the Bear southward along the coast of Norway for forty minutes when the Phantom showed up. Far left above, a Soviet Bear D maritime surveillance aircraft. The Bear hunts for the carrier battle group with its Big Bulge radar (seen on the lower fuselage where the wings join). The Bear passes on targeting data to airborne, surface, and subsurface long-range missile shooters. In the event of a conflict, the Tomcat's job is to prevent the Bear from getting close enough to do that. Far left below, a VF-102 F-14A escorts a Norwegian F-16 during Ocean Safari 85 just off the coast of Norway. *Dave Parsons*

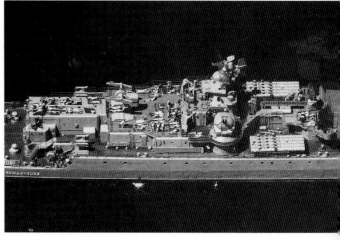

USS *America* steams inside Norway's Vestfjord during Ocean Safari 85. *US Navy*. Above right, a TARPS photo of Soviet cruiser anchored just north of the Gulf of Sidra in 1986. The sailors seem more interested in catching a few rays than monitoring the activities of the three carrier battle groups steaming nearby. *US Navy*. Far right above, carrier aviators fly routinely in heavy weather and rough seas, which along with the carrier landing is what makes them unique. *Joe Higgins*. Far right below, the dramatic effect achieved when a supersonic Tomcat makes a low pass. The disturbance on the water's surface is from the supersonic shock wave. *US Navy*

at-sea periods. A few of the officers were celebrating the end of a training exercise off the coast of Cuba by chugging "bug juice" (Kool-Aid) and munching popcorn. The stereo was cranked a bit above normal levels with vintage Beatles singing "Birthday." Everyone in the room began singing along with a fervor that periods at sea generated. Suddenly the door opened.

The junior officers froze as a silver-haired figure dressed in well-pressed khakis entered. It was the captain. At sea, no one wielded more power. Ted reached up and flicked the power switch on the amplifier and the entire system ground to an abrupt halt. He hated to secure it that way because it could wreck the fidelity of the tape at the point it stopped, but the situation called for instant silence.

"What the hell is that you gents are listening to? Punk rock?" Ted couldn't believe the captain didn't recognize the Beatles. Christ, he was a junior officer himself when the *White Album* came out. "Anyone in here got their hair parted down the middle?" referring to the Navy adage started in the seventies that sailors that parted their hair down the middle were also drug users. The lieutenants laughed politely and rose from their chairs, still in semi-shock from this unorthodox intrusion.

"We're just trying to unwind a bit, Captain," Ted managed.

"No problem there, gents. Just keep it down a bit. Carry on." With that he was gone.

"I guess everybody the captain's age who liked the Beatles is out of the Navy by now," Lieutenant Jim "Slime" Cook said, sinking back into his chair.

"I guess . . . Punk rock? How does a guy get to be so out-of-it?" Ted wondered out loud.

"Face it, Ted. The man got where he is because he is a fantastic judge of character and he knows a punk when he sees one."

"Hey, dudes. I might be a lot of things but I am definitely not a punk." In a crowd of tactical aviators this was the perfectly wrong thing to say.

The chant began. The other guys formed a circle around Ted screaming, "Punk! Punk! Punk!"

He'd worn that moniker for almost two years now and was used to it. In fact, his real name sounded foreign in the unlikely event that someone used it. Punk had learned from experience that seasoned aviators without callsigns were either assholes or boring.

Later, the skipper of Stephens' squadron and a nugget radar intercept officer have a hostile, airborne encounter with an Iranian F-4 Phantom, which shoots a missile at them. Chasing the F-4, the skipper makes a crucial error. The ensuing dialogue eventually generates a callsign for his radar intercept officer.

They rolled out just over a mile and a half behind the Iranian. The Phantom had a big speed advantage and was opening in a hurry. "One time, babe! One time!" Commander Campbell was a raging madman, not cold and calculating. He jammed the weapons select toggle switch located on the stick down in an attempt to select "Sidewinder" instead of "Sparrow." Unfortunately, the skipper's hysteria got the best of him and he switched the weapons select past "Sidewinder" down to "Guns." He squeezed the trigger. The "bbbrrrrraaaapppp" of the gun mocked them like Islamic laughter and the bullets fell into the ocean.

"I think he's too far away for guns, Skipper," Paul suggested.

"No goddam shit, Einstein!" The skipper was livid. He successfully selected Sidewinder the second time and fired. It was too late. The Phantom had used the time to get out of range. The Sidewinder followed its little bullet brothers into the sea.

After the F-14 returns to the carrier, Paul and his fellow junior officers, Punk among them, watch the cockpit film of the fiasco. The junior officers commiserate with Paul, who wrongly received the brunt of the skipper's frustration.

The aviators in the room sat transfixed as the tape rolled. There were a few gasps and more than one "sshhiieett" expressed as the television showed the F-4 shooting the missile. The abbreviations at the bottom of the head-up display documented that the skipper had indeed switched from SP to G, vice SW. Punk had to force himself not to laugh when the tape got to the "no goddam shit, Einstein" part.

"Ladies and gentlemen, we have a callsign," Punk said. The rest of the room must have been thinking the same thing because the group broke into laughter. It was true. Paul was no longer just-plain-Paul. A pooch was screwed and he was present. From now on, he would be known as "Einstein."

Enter the Nugget

The aircrews discover that the rites are not yet over when they walk in the door of their new squadron. They are now bona fide "nuggets," the name given to aviators on their first cruise. The term "nugget" is roughly analogous to being a freshman—only time and requisite seasoning can make the name go away. Their callsign is scrutinized and it will either stick or be modified. They also find the familiar hit board in their new squadron as well.

A squadron tries to pull in all its new nuggets around the beginning of a turn-

around cycle to give the freshmen time to work into the squadron routine and come up to speed in time for the eventual sea deployment. Sometimes, however, the RAG delivers a "full-up round" and nuggets may join a squadron already at sea. A fighter squadron is continually in a state of flux as it repeats the cycle of "working up" for deployment, deploying, returning, and standing down prior to working up again.

Personnel constantly join and depart. Over a three-year period, 100 percent of the personnel will turn over. The only constant is change. Flexibility is the name of the game. As a result, there is a perceptible atmosphere whether you're deployed or ashore: You feel constant anticipation, and you wait for something to happen at the last moment.

When a crisis involving US interests breaks out anywhere in the world, the oft-repeated question from the White House to the inner halls of the joint chiefs of staff is, "Where are the carriers?" An aircraft carrier with her ninety-aircraft air wing can be called upon to sortie to virtually any part of the world as long as there is a navigable waterway. To keep

carriers and squadrons ready for combat and at the same time balance needs for refitting and personnel turnover, stand-downs of roughly a year between deployments are necessary. Actually, the squadron hardly stands down at all. After a deployment, the squadron maps out a turnaround training cycle that will bring all its aviators to peak proficiency. A squadron will participate in its own in-house training as well as major events such as weapons deployment to NAS Fallon and carrier qualification prior to each time at sea.

FFARP

During the turnaround period, each fighter squadron goes through FFARP (Fleet Fighter Air Combat Maneuvering Readiness Program), which is run by the resident adversaries, the VF-43 Challengers. Topgun gives one aircrew from a squadron at a time a graduate education in the fighter business. FFARP involves the entire squadron. If a comparison had to be made, FFARP would be a masters level. Developed originally by VF-43

The intent expressions on the faces of these landing signal officers (LSO) as they watch an aircraft land underscore the seriousness of their task. Right, an aircrew pulls the seemingly endless alert duty. Far right above, the fighter's best friend is the KA-6D, which allows the Tomcat to stay aloft indefinitely. Here, a KA-6D Tanker comes aboard with five external fuel tanks. Far right below, the EA-6B's canopies are impregnated with gold to protect the occupants from the side effects of their own jamming. *Dave Parsons*

during the dogfight-training renaissance of the 1970s, FFARP is the greatest contributor to honing a squadron's air-to-air combat readiness.

FFARP begins with the squadron attending a series of lectures ranging from air-to-air tactics to weapons performance to an update on the air-to-air threat. The flying begins with one-versus-one dissimilar sorties against the different types of aircraft flown by VF-43. Today, that means the F-16N, F-5, and several models of the A-4, including the much vaunted Super Fox version. The air-combat sorties are all flown on the Tactical Aircrew Combat Training System, which is an instrumented range that enables aircraft weapons to be employed in virtual real-time on a computer that assesses their performance. The range, which was initially known as the Air Combat Maneuvering Range, is one of the most significant advances in air-combat training. For debriefing, the entire engagement is available for playback and is presented on a three-dimensional display. Many times, an aircrew cannot remember all the intricate maneuvers of a dynamic fight, which is why the recording of the flight serves as a valuable tool. It is especially useful in multi-participant fights. As it is often said, the playback eliminates the old "first to the blackboard or one with the loudest voice wins" debrief.

After the basic one-versus-one series, the squadron progresses to section work pitting two Tomcats against a variety of threats. The culmination is division tactics in which two sections of Tomcats take on mixed formations of bandits. Adversary formations, tactics, and weapons simulated are similar to those the Tomcats might face on deployment. Because air combat maneuvering fuel costs are high and availability of adversary aircraft limited, FFARP is extremely cost-effective and gives the squadron the most for their training dollars. By the end of the three-week syllabus, the entire squadron's proficiency is honed to a fine edge.

The majority of adversary pilots flying with VF-43 are just off their first tour in Tomcats and are intimately familiar with the strengths and weaknesses of the aircraft. Once up to speed as an adversary, they can be a formidable opponent. As most will point out, however, their objective is to lose. If an F-14

The aircraft carrier is a city at sea that never sleeps. *US Navy*. Right, carriers and their aircraft must be ready for action even in a snowstorm. *Dana Potts*

they will have to use off the boat. Fallon deployments have been a big part of turn-around training for years. Fallon's graduate-level "Strike U" is central to molding an air wing into an effective fighting organization. The introduction of more sophisticated threats and the increased variety of sophisticated weapons carried by the air wing have brought the need for advanced complex tactics. Fallon is where these are put into practice. Fallon's advanced Tactical Aircrew Combat Training System range can handle up to thirty-five aircraft.

At Fallon, the air wing's strike planners map out and execute a variety of strikes involving virtually every capability the air wing has against land targets. The highly professional staff at Strike U monitors and instructs while the wide-open terrain of the Nevada desert offers ample room for the air wing to execute a host of scenarios using live ordnance. VFA-127 is based at Fallon and provides A-4 and F-5 adversary support to the visiting air wings.

After Fallon, the air wing is ready to go to sea.

Life on the Boat

The deployment of a carrier for its six months at sea is the culmination of all the enormous resources devoted to bringing the entire ship and air wing team to combat-ready status. For a fighter squadron, the challenge is to bring all the assigned aircrews to peak proficiency in the squadron's assigned mission areas and to operate flawlessly around the boat.

Before that deployment occurs, the carrier-air wing team goes through a series of short periods at sea collectively referred to as "workups." Formal periods of training at sea include Refresher Training and Advanced Phase where the carrier embarks a carrier group staff to coordinate the training of the entire battle group of ships with the carrier. East Coast carriers operate just offshore during this time, sometimes steaming to the extensive ranges off the coast of Puerto Rico for fleet exercises. Some carriers participate in a North Atlantic Treaty Organization (NATO) exercise in the North Sea, spending six to eight weeks at sea and operating in Norwegian fjords. Workups span the better part of a year prior to the six-month deployment. During

aircrew can go through the FFARP syllabus and come out on top, they have probably already flown against the toughest opponents they should ever have to face.

NAS Fallon

A major operation in the turnaround training cycle is the air wing weapons deployment to NAS Fallon, Nevada. This is the first time the air wing assembles as a whole since the previous cruise. A typical air wing is made up of nine squadrons that are from five bases spread across the country. At NAS Fallon they come together and work on integrated tactics

Alert Launch

"Now launch the alert fighters! Now launch the alert fighters!"

The call over the loudspeakers sparks action on the flight deck. Two alert Tomcats sit manned and ready with hoses and cables hooked up. Before the loudspeaker finishes the call, the canopies begin closing with a hiss and the external air hose snakes to life. The routine is well-practiced so words are clipped and few. The engines begin winding up almost immediately and as soon as one is turning, the generators come on line.

Fingers dance over the consoles in both cockpits bringing the Tomcat to life. Both pilot and radar intercept officer exchange a series of hand signals with the maintenance personnel on the flight deck below them indicating status of various systems and responding to different checks. The yellow shirts and blue shirts stand just outside their circle waiting their turn. With a thumbs up from the crew, the director begins his wordless communication, flashing hand signals in rapid succession to the pilot and the blue shirts under his control. The chocks and chains come off and the director signals the pilot to taxi the thirty-ton Tomcat.

The catapult crew stands waiting and the Tomcat is passed into position director by director at the beginning of the steam-venting track. As the nose kneels, the wings start forward into the takeoff position. As they stop at the twenty-degree position, the flaps and slats start down. Troubleshooters flanking the aircraft quickly do their routine and take position for the launch.

The director calls for full power and the Tomcat lurches as the catapult shuttle is put into tension. The catapult officer is in control and calls for burner. The nozzles expand through the five stages and the Tomcat shakes as it strains to be released from its restraints. Salutes are exchanged and the catapult officer signals for launch.

The catapult fires, propelling thirty tons of fighter to 120 knots in less than three seconds. The pilot throws the Tomcat into an airshow-quality left turn—not to impress, but to get to the intercept vector in the shortest amount of time possible. The Tomcat is no longer restrained and is accelerating faster than a scalded cat. Normal rules don't apply for alert launches. The flight deck-bound personnel who launched the Tomcat watch it straighten out on the vector heading and haul the nose up like it's going for the moon. In the rear cockpit, the radar intercept officer brings more systems on line, checking out the weapons system and missiles.

An actual alert launch is exciting. The goal is to get off the deck as quickly as possible. Friendly rivalry builds between the carrier's sister squadrons. Each squadron maintains one Alert 5 bird and it is a point of pride to be first off the deck. Watching the flight-deck teamwork is like watching a well-executed series of football plays culminating in a touchdown.

The Tomcat is the battle group's first line of defense. As an interceptor, it has no equal. Maintaining combat air patrol stations or intercepting incoming aircraft off an alert launch hundreds of miles from the carrier is a routine event. Even without in-flight refueling, the Tomcat's range is unprecedented. A common alert launch for the Tomcat is to pick up a pair of Soviet Bear D aircraft and escort them as long as they remain within a circle of several hundred miles from the carrier. A standard alert package is two Tomcats. Since Bears usually travel in pairs, each Tomcat takes its own Bear.

To be ready to handle the task of interception, Tomcat crews stand varying levels of alert. The highest, Alert 5, is stood with the crew strapped in the cockpit, day or night, wet or dry, cold or hot, pitching or steady deck. The Alert 5 crew is backed up by a fully dressed Alert 15 crew in the ready room, who have an assigned jet to go to should the Alert 5 be launched. They in turn are backed by Alert 30 and Alert 60 crews. Every two hours, the Alert 5 crew is relieved by the Alert 15 crew and so on.

The excitement of a launch punctuates hour upon hour of standing alert duty. In the North Atlantic, at two in the morning with seventy knots of wind over a pitching deck, no one wants the thrill of an alert launch. Sleep is impossible while strapped to an ejection seat regardless of weather. The most highly prized alert launches are the ones that end up with a Bear or other Soviet aircraft escort.

For East Coast carriers, the annual North Atlantic NATO exercises usually mean a foray through the Greenland, Iceland, United Kingdom (GIUK) gap, Bear territory. The farther you go up the Norwegian coast, the more Russian reaction you get.

Alert launches aren't the only times a Tomcat flies close to other aircraft. Wherever a carrier travels, it seems to run into unusual aircraft: West German transports in the Indian Ocean, Bears just outside Norfolk, Virginia, and airliners just off

Libya's coast in the midst of prowling missile-armed Tomcats.

Not everyone likes to be intercepted. The solitary patrol aircraft seem to like the company, but airliners get skittish when other aircraft approach, which makes interception tricky, especially when the carrier is asking for a tail number. Airliners are usually not worth the trouble. The television camera set (TCS) does the job nicely with the proper aspect, without getting passengers excited about a missile-armed fighter flying alongside. Any fighter-type aircraft—for example, an F-15 out of Holland—usually wants to "play" (ACM). You can't take very good pictures pulling six Gs. I've got a smashed camera to prove it.

The Bears are probably the easiest. We know why they are there, and they know what we're all about. I imagine they enjoy a little company during their thirteen-hour missions. The tail gunners politely tip their cannon skyward. The tales of what crews of each side display to each other are legendary. Soviet crews hold up Pepsi bottles, *Playboy*, and cameras. US crews wearing monster masks hold up *Playboy*, or signs.

I carried a sign that said, "Smile Kapitan, smile" in Russian. It was taken from a well-known Soviet Navy song. (I asked a friend who knows the language to make up "Smile, Comrade" so I could display it on a sign before I took a picture. He had suggested the Kapitan version and even sang me the song.) The first time I displayed the sign, a Bear tail gunner laughed and nodded his head. I guess they must sing it all the time. He motioned for us to move forward so the cockpit crew could see. In our normal escort position, only the tail gunner sees us. It's a long way from the tail to the nose on a Bear, but we made it, giving the big wing a wide berth on the way. There was a pack of crewmen up there, all crowded up to the window smiling and snapping photographs.

Signs go both ways. In 1984, the crew of an Iranian P-3 held up a sign, but try as we might, we couldn't read it. We took it to be friendly as they were all smiling and waving. I guess you would try to be friendly if you were in an unarmed aircraft with an F-14 armed to the teeth on your wing, despite what your leader might say. Most Iranian crews were Navy-trained, so maybe it was a message to someone in Pensacola.

this time the nuggets become accustomed to life at sea, particularly the demands of around-the-clock flight operations, alerts, general-quarters drills, wearing of gas masks, and on- and off-loading of their possessions.

When the time comes to deploy, the squadron packs up lock, stock, and barrel, cleaning out their quarters at Oceana. Everything is packed in footlocker-sized collapsible steel "cruise boxes." If it won't fit into a cruise box, it's wrapped in bubble wrap and taped with silver "ordie" tape before loading in a truck for transport to the ship.

Aboard the ship, the squadron moves into spaces assigned to its various workcenters and the ready room, which becomes the aircrews' office, briefing room, and living room.

The staterooms allocated to the aircrews vary in size and are assigned by seniority. They range in size from one-man rooms (reserved for commanding and executive officers) and two-

A view through the twin tails of a Tomcat spotted on the deck edge of a carrier. Aircrews must be extremely careful preflighting the top of the Tomcat when it is parked this way as a loss of footing could result in a sudden slide through the tails and over the side. It's a long way to the water below. *Dave Parsons*

man rooms for lieutenant commanders (sometimes senior lieutenants as well) to a mix of various sized bunkrooms. The bunkrooms are usually called "JO Jungles" due to their typical occupancy by junior officers and are four-, six-, eight-, and even twelve-man rooms. All rooms feature a steel "rack" (Navy term for bed) aligned with the ship's keel. Each occupant has an individual desk and a wall locker with drawers. All the occupants share a sink and medicine cabinet (six-man and higher have two). During the workup cycle, the occupants make them habitable for the impending cruise, usually installing rugs and privacy curtains. No respectable jungle is complete without a color television, video cassette recorder, compact disc or cassette player, and a Nintendo game. The larger jungles are popular gathering spots since they have the most floor space of any of the rooms and the most impressive entertainment systems.

During workups, carrier landing practice is of major importance. A nugget's greatest challenge is proving himself at the back end of the boat. Rather than simply qualifying, he finds grades for all his passes conspicuously posted in the ready room alongside the other pilots' on a "Greenie Board." Every pass is viewed on a closed-circuit television system (called the Pilot's Landing Aid Television or PLAT) and recorded for playback. The nugget is soon aware that the captain of the ship, the air wing commander, his deputy, and just about everyone else in the chain of command are watching his passes. During a nugget's first time out on the boat, the ready room audience's attention is always focused on the PLAT at night when the nugget comes aboard. If the pass isn't pretty, not only will he hear about it and get to watch it, but it will stand out on the Greenie Board for all to see.

Once the deployment finally begins, the idea of six months at sea doesn't seem as bad as the disruptive out and in schedule of workups that strains family relations. The deployment, which is typically referred to as "cruise," is almost a relief, especially from the daily general quarters drills and wearing of gas masks associated with workups. Some cruises are called "loveboat cruises" when the world situation is relaxed and the carrier has a frequent port schedule in such desirable ports as Monte Carlo, Malaga, Naples, Rhodes, Athens, Haifa, and other Mediterranean ports. Other cruises

are brutal with over 100 days at sea. Many carriers steamed to the Indian Ocean during the late 1970s and early 1980s spending over 100 days on station off Iran with few port calls.

Aside from its considerable war-fighting potential, below decks, the carrier possesses the resources of a small town. To support the roughly 5,000 personnel, the carrier has a hospital, a post office, gymnasiums, several "restaurants," fire and police departments, a dental clinic, stores, banking facilities, a television studio, a bakery, barber shops, a photo lab, a machine shop, a garage, and a whole range of repair services. The carrier is open for business twenty-four hours a day so it is not quiet and peaceful like a small town, especially during flight operations. A thirty-ton Tomcat slamming onto the flight deck and stopping in a few hundred feet makes a lot of noise. All hands including the nugget must adapt to this environment, which will be home for at least six months.

On cruise, aircrews live to fly. It is a tremendous release from the confines and boredom of the ship. A cat shot is never dull and while day landings are basically fun, the night landings can really get your attention. By midcruise, the nuggets are well seasoned and are no longer under constant scrutiny every time they come aboard. Their Greenie Board doesn't look like a Christmas tree selection of colors either. A lot of flying on cruise is called "hanging on the blades"—throttled back and flying slow to conserve fuel. By throttling back during the airborne cycle time, a little gas can be saved to allow for a short period of "bumping heads" prior to recovery.

A normal cruise features participation with foreign countries in a variety of exercises, which gives aircrews a chance to operate over land and pit their skills against other aircrews in dissimilar aircraft. Occasionally a small detachment of aircraft flies ashore for operations with a foreign air force such as in France. The carrier's primary mission while deployed is presence, which can be exciting when conflict occurs, as it has off Lebanon, Libya, and Saudi Arabia. Cruise can also be boring and drawn out when presence requires a carrier to maintain position near a potential hot spot because training and port calls are constrained.

The end of cruise is always welcomed as the squadron looks forward to being reunited

with loved ones and longs for the good old USA. As the carrier approaches the East Coast, the entire air wing flies off in one day. As each squadron has more aircrew than cockpits, not all aircrews get a fly-off seat. Seats are assigned by seniority, so many nuggets do not make the cut. Each squadron assembles after takeoff and flies over Oceana in formation prior to landing. The nugget has now arrived and has, no doubt, a few patches to sew on his flight jacket as well as a few tales to tell at the club to the eager RAG trainees.

Chapter 3

Tomcats in the Storm

Western Iraq, January 17, 1991: F-14A Tomcats from the USS *John F. Kennedy* push across the border in a fighter sweep clearing the strike route of Iraqi interceptors so the A-6E Intruders and A-7E Corsairs can proceed to H-2 airfield unhindered. Minutes later, another sweep of USS *Saratoga*-based F-14A Plus Tomcats would do the same a little farther to the west for their F/A-18 Hornets and A-6E Intruders assigned to hit the H-3 airfield complex.

As sixty aircraft left their US Air Force tankers over central Iraq and switched from their tanker control frequencies to the strike control net, they had the first indications of possible Iraqi aerial resistance. Airborne Warning and Control System (AWACS) aircraft were "painting" several Iraqi combat air patrols in the immediate vicinity of the H-2 and H-3 airfields. It looked like a showdown was ahead. At dawn, *Kennedy*-based Tomcats executed a fighter sweep in the same area hoping to catch Iraqi fighters in the air, but returned disappointed. There had been reports of scattered Iraqi fighter activity since the first bombs and Tomahawk missiles struck at 0300, with no indication of a concerted attempt to challenge the allied armada's scores of forays across the border.

The aircraft patrolling near H-2 and H-3 appeared to be the first Iraqi attempt to lash back at the allied aircraft. The Tomcats were ready. Each carried two long-range Phoenix missiles, three medium-range Sparrow mis-

siles, two short-range Sidewinder missiles, and a full load of 20mm ammo for its Vulcan cannon. The Phoenix had yet to see combat use by the US Navy, but the Iraqis had firsthand experience with its effectiveness during their ten-year war with Iran. Iranian Tomcats used their Phoenix missile with deadly results against Iraqi fighters. The Navy had fired both Sidewinder and Sparrow missiles in the 1981 and 1989 incidents with Libya resulting in two Su-22 Fitters and two MiG-23 Floggers downed with no loss to the Navy crews. The Tomcat aircrews crossing from Saudi airspace into Iraq were sure that the Iraqi fighter pilots were well acquainted with the Tomcat's reputation.

As the lead Tomcats closed to Phoenix firing range, the Iraqi fighters abandoned their patrol stations, fleeing east, north, and west to remain clear of the Phoenix's lethal envelope. It was as if the Tomcats' powerful AWG-9 radars were actually repelling the hostile fighters, much to the chagrin of the Tomcat crews, but heartwarming to the strike aircraft. The western fleeing MiG-21s stumbled into two *Saratoga* F/A-18 Hornets that were carrying both air-to-air and air-to-ground ordnance. A *Saratoga* E-2 Hawkeye called out the bandits to the Hornet pilots who quickly selected air-to-air mode on their weapons control systems, positioned themselves for radar locks on the MiGs, and dispatched both with Sparrow missiles. The sweeping A Plus Tomcats had already passed by and were not in a position to engage. Both the *Saratoga* and *Kennedy* strike

One of the many Desert Storm patches designed by the participating squadrons. Left, a strike group in the process of refuelling over Saudi Arabia prior to a strike on Iraq. US Air Force tankers travelled in cells of four to five aircraft stacked vertically and in trail. The KA-6D tanker to the right of the KC-135 had launched early, met up with the tanker and topped off. When the strike group arrived, it was ready to pass fuel as well, which multiplied the number of hoses available, speeding transfer. After the strike group detached, the KA-6D proceeded north to wait for the strikers. *Dave Parsons*

Battle Force Red Sea steams in formation off the western coast of Saudi Arabia during Desert Storm. Commanded by Rear Admiral Riley Mixson, the task force included the carriers USS *John F. Kennedy*, USS *Saratoga*, and USS *America*, along with four AEGIS class cruisers and other surface combatants. This photograph was taken shortly before USS *America* left the Red Sea to join Naval forces in the Persian Gulf. *US Navy.* Right, a VF-32 F-14A Tomcat and VA-75 A-6E Intruder practice low-level flight over the Saudi Arabian desert. *Dave Parsons*

Aircrews and flight deck personnel conducted regular drills on the use of chemical protective gear during Desert Shield and Storm. *Craig Dugan.* Below, Gypsy 200 flies along Saudi Arabia's western coast. *Dave Parsons*

groups were able to release their ordnance unhindered.

Despite a large number of airborne fighters, the Iraqis chose not to confront the Tomcats head-on. As the strike groups headed south, the fleeing Iraqi fighters returned to their stations. Two MiG-29 Fulcrums started to close on the trailing element of the *Kennedy* strike group, which was composed of two EA-6B Prowlers and their escort of two Tomcats. The Tomcats' job was to stay close to the Prowlers to keep the Fulcrums from closing in to be an immediate threat. As the miles ticked by, the Tomcats prepared to turn and confront the closing bandits. The Tomcats waited for the Prowlers to reach the safety of the Saudi border or the Fulcrums to get too close for comfort.

With less than a minute left until the Prowlers reached the border, a US Air Force strike force crossed the Tomcats' path making its way toward Mudaysis and al Asad airfields. The lead F-15 Eagles had been alerted to the presence of the Fulcrums and two sweepers were heading in their direction at Mach 1.5.

The two Eagles passed the Tomcats and, before they reached the Tomcats' five o'clock position, launched AIM-7 Sparrows that downed both Fulcrums. Thus ended the Tomcats' greatest opportunity for aerial combat on the first day of Operation Desert Storm.

As the days of Desert Storm rumbled past, it became apparent the Iraqi air force was not going to be the challenge to allied air supremacy that it could have been—either by choice, ineffective tactics, or by permanent and temporary degradation of the crucial Iraqi ground control system by electronic jamming and destruction of radar installations. Indeed, after the hardened aircraft bunkers showed themselves to be no protection against the I-2000 bomb, the majority of Iraqi air force activity was low-and-fast escape flights to Iran. Only the US Air Force and Royal Saudi Arabian Air Force F-15 Eagles met with repeated success against the few Iraqi fighters that did venture forth (either to battle or run to Iran).

It is wrong to draw a straight-line analysis of the relative effectiveness of both fighters based solely on the Eagle's kill ratio of seventeen victories against no losses compared to the Tomcat's sole victory against a helicopter and no losses. To those who flew either aircraft during Desert Storm, the first and most telling argument against comparison is the nature of missions flown by each aircraft. Eagles were assigned to border and in-country combat-air-patrol stations from the start to finish of the conflict, which was where most engagements

A VF-32 Tomcat climbs vertically with six AIM-54 Phoenix missiles. The majority of Tomcats flew with mixed loads of Phoenix, Sparrow, and Sidewinder missiles. *Dave Parsons.* Lower left, missile armed F-14A Plus Tomcats pack the bow of USS *Saratoga* after returning from combat missions. *US Navy.* Far left, returning from a combat mission over Iraq late in the conflict, two VF-32 Tomcats make a low pass over spectacular reefs bordering the western coast of Saudi Arabia as they head home to USS *John F. Kennedy. Dave Parsons*

occurred. After the initiation of the ground war, Tomcats were assigned one in-country air-patrol station. Both Red Sea- and Persian Gulf-based Tomcats flew in defense of the fleet, and did not encounter any Iraqi aircraft. The Tomcats that did go in-country were tied to strike groups and could only engage bandits if the bandits directly challenged the strike group. Most strike groups spent less than an hour in-country limiting opportunity for encountering Iraqi fighters. US Air Force fighters patrolled over Iraq around the clock. This gave Eagles both a mission advantage (freedom to attack bandits) and increased opportunity in exposure time (at least five times as much).

As the opening to this chapter reveals, the Iraqis chose not to engage Tomcats, which

During Desert Storm, an Air Force KC-135 refuels a group of Oceana-based Tomcats over the Saudi Arabian desert. Typical strike missions involved taking on fuel before and after going into Iraq. In addition to the big Air Force tankers, the Navy used KA-6Ds as hose multipliers and stationed S-3Bs as emergency tankers near the carriers. *Dave Parsons*. Lower left, the Tomcat provided combat air patrol around the clock for the fleet during Desert Shield and Desert Storm. The lonely vigil of flying hours of racetrack patterns over a single spot as the powerful AWG-9 radar searched out contacts is vital and often taken for granted. *Dave Parsons*. Far left, a plane captain cleans and polishes the canopy of a USS *Saratoga*-based F-14A Plus Tomcat. Aircrews are very particular about the condition of the canopy since even a smudge of dirt can interfere with their visual scan by distracting the eye, which is looking for bogies roughly the same size. *US Navy*

points out a more subtle and often overlooked measure of effectiveness—that of deterrence. The Tomcat's mission was to get the strike group to and from the target without interference from hostile fighters. If this can be accomplished by mere presence, then the mission is successful. All fighter pilots hanker for the opportunity to shoot down enemy fighters. But if the enemy fighters attack the strike group and impede or break down its cohesiveness—or shoot down a friendly aircraft—then the fighter mission is unsuccessful, no matter how many enemy fighters are shot down. While only an interview with the Iraqi pilots can reveal their true reluctance to challenge the Tomcat, Navy aircrews saw the results and referred with great fondness to the Tomcat's radar as the "MiG repeller." The question to ask is what would have happened if the Tomcats had not been there?

Perhaps the correct view is that both aircraft were part of the coalition team and both did their jobs admirably. It is a shallow view that compares the two aircraft solely on the basis of aerial victories. The Tomcat crews would have liked a close encounter with the

Above and right, VF-32 F-14s race low over the Saudi desert. *Dave Parsons.*

Iraqi air force, but can be proud of the totally successful deterrent role they played.

Smile, Baghdad

Another role in which the Tomcat excelled was that of photo reconnaissance. Introduced to the Tomcat community in the late 1970s, the role of photo recon has been performed by one of the two Tomcat squadrons assigned to each Tomcat-equipped air wing. By carrying the 1,800 pound Tactical Aerial Reconnaissance Pod System (TARPS), the Tomcat fulfills the role vacated by the departure of the RF-8 Crusader and RA-5 Vigilante. At first, TARPS was not seen to be a player in the Desert Storm aerial campaign due to the presence of many dedicated aerial reconnaissance assets in theater, notably the RF-4 Phantoms, TR-1, and OV-1 Mohawks. The need for integral Navy bomb damage assessment and the intensive counter-Scud effort brought TARPS into the forefront.

While photo recon aircraft have traditionally been "alone, unarmed, and unafraid"

A night launch on USS *John F. Kennedy. Bill Lipski.* Left a tow tractor aboard *USS Saratoga. US Navy*

with few historical deviations, the Tomcat configured with the TARPS pod retains its weapons capability and does not need fighter escort for its mission. This made TARPS a cost-effective asset to Desert Storm planners. Another plus was the Tomcat's range in-country, which exceeded all other assets and allowed coverage of hundreds of miles of roads and bomb damage assessment of many targets in a single mission with a single pre- and post-mission aerial refueling.

Tomcats were used in high-risk missions to obtain crucial photos of al Asad airfield and al Qaim super phosphate plant that has SA-6, SA-2, and SA-3 surface-to-air-missile sites

ringing the target. The TARPS Tomcats were the principal collection platform for the counter-Scud effort, flying daily missions throughout western and central Iraq covering known Scud operating areas. In late February, a TARPS crew discovered a major Scud missile assembly area that resulted in three days of strike missions by Navy and Air Force aircraft.

Tomcats flew from the decks of five of the aircraft carriers participating in Desert Storm: USS *Kennedy*, USS *Saratoga*, USS *Roosevelt*, USS *America*, and USS *Ranger*. America-based Tomcats saw action in both the Red Sea and Persian Gulf. Tomcats flew the endless and mostly thankless job of combat air patrol for the fleet, guarding against Exocet-equipped Iraqi aircraft, which had terrorized the Persian Gulf for so long and were capable of striking the many coalition ships cruising in both the Red Sea and Persian Gulf. It is perhaps the simple deterrent of having Phoenix-equipped

Tomcats aloft that kept the Iraqis from pursuing this option.

When the ground offensive began in late February, Tomcats were stretched to the limits of their endurance flying eight-hour combat air patrol missions to protect the ground forces from aerial attack. Combat air patrol stations were manned with both USAF F-15 Eagles and F-14 Tomcats alternating in huge "lanes" of responsibility that stretched well beyond the forward advance of coalition forces. Tomcats were assigned the "Bong" station, which was east of Baghdad. Here, Tomcats from both bodies of water met as they relieved each other. The mission called for three sections of Tomcats at a time to fly a demanding three-hour patrol inside Iraq before relief by another set of Tomcats. Operating often to the northeast of Baghdad, the Tomcats had to steer clear of numerous surface-to-air-missile sites in order to perform their missions. The Iraqis chose not

Lieutenant Commanders Drew "Bluto" Brugal and Dave "Hey Joe" Parsons man Gypsy 204 on the first day of the Desert Storm air campaign. *"Red" Pamperin.* Left, Lieutenant Major "Beav" Murray (right) goes over fine points of flying procedures in the Red Sea with Lieutenant Rich "Kid" Cornwall while standing Alert 15 duty in the VF-32 ready room during Desert Storm. *Dave Parsons.* Far left, a Tomcat is taxied into position on catapult 1 aboard USS *Saratoga*. *US Navy*

73

to run the gauntlet formed by the Tomcats, which prevented the Iraqis from attacking the ground troops and from escaping to Iran.

The Tomcats flown in Desert Storm were the result of nearly twenty years of experience with the aircraft. Unlike the Phantom, which saw its replacement (the Tomcat) flying barely ten years after its entry onto fleet service, the Tomcat has shown great stamina since its fleet intro in 1973. The most advanced Tomcat in Desert Storm, the F-14A Plus (now called F-14B), flew off the *Saratoga* with VF-74 and VF-103. The A Plus features two 29,000-pound thrust General Electric F110 engines, which is a substantial boost in power over the straight A's two 20,000-pound thrust Pratt & Whitney TF-30s. The A Plus also has the more advanced ALR-67 Radar Homing and Warning (RHAW) suite, which is much more capable than the aged ALR-45/50 gear equipping the F-14A.

All Tomcats received the ASW-27C datalink systems prior to Desert Storm, allowing interface with the fighter-to-fighter datalink feature resident in the Tape 115A software. This feature received universal praise from aircrews and was a major contributor to situational awareness and coordination during large strikes. The ability for all "participating" Tomcats to "see" each other on their respective Tactical Information Displays and query information as well as transmit and receive radar contacts between each other was a significant new feature.

TARPS Tomcats were able to enhance their survivability by mounting an Expanded Chaff Adaptor in the left forward Phoenix rail with 120 rounds of chaff or flares. The right rail could carry the ALQ-167 jamming pod. All TARPS squadrons were equipped with long-range cameras allowing greater standoff or higher altitudes that reduced the threat from antiaircraft fire and surface-to-air missiles.

Although the Tomcat's AWG-9 radar is basically the same hardware as originally introduced, the software is continuously and routinely upgraded to keep pace with the threat and incorporate features requested from the fleet operators. This capability has allowed the Tomcat, as the first member of the fourth-generation fighters, to remain current with changes in electronic counter countermeasures and remain viable with the latest fourth-generation fighters. The radar's TARPS

Refuelling probe doors were often damaged in bouts with the KC-135. *Craig Dugan.* Below, a VF-32 Tomcat refuels from a KC-135 inside Iraq in the course of flying unprecedented eight hour combat air patrol missions during the ground campaign. *Dave Parsons.* Far left, a VF-14 Tomcat on combat air patrol in the Red Sea takes on fuel from a Kansas Air National Guard KC-135. To refuel Navy aircraft, which use the probe-and-drogue system, the flying boom must be configured with a specially designed basket. *US Navy*

submode was recently updated to allow it to run concurrently with the air-to-air mode.

Although the Tomcat was originally designed to carry bombs, a variety of reasons have kept the bombs off the aircraft. Bombs will now be carried (none were in Desert Storm) and all fleet squadrons are in the process of receiving the bombracks and training to accomplish this mission. The Tomcat can carry four Mk-83 or Mk-84 LD bombs under the fuselage with ease and at high speed, making it a strike fighter with a large load. Future improvements could allow the Tomcat to carry the full range of "smart" weaponry.

Although the F-14D is under limited production, its future seems cloudy as the Navy debates the composition of its future air wings. The Tomcat's sophistication and capability carry a high price tag and, with the diminished and perceived threat, the Tomcat may have to step aside for the F/A-18E and F/A-18F models, which are less capable but cheaper.

Tomcats refuel as the sun goes down. Fighters were expected to provide round-the-clock air patrols, so night aerial refuelling became routine for both tanker and fighter crews. *Dave Parsons*

Down in Iraq:
Lieutenant Devon Jones' Survival Story
By Peter Mersky

Nobody expects to be shot down, but because of survival training, every aircrewman is better prepared for that possibility, and his chances of coming out are high.

Lieutenant Devon Jones and his RIO, Lieutenant Larry Slade, manned their F-14B for an escort mission on the fourth day of Desert Storm. This would be the first time that the two VF-103 aviators had crossed the beach. They launched from USS *Saratoga* (CV-60) with their EA-6B and headed for their target where the Prowler crew would shoot a HARM.

It was still dark when the two aircraft turned away from the target after the Prowler's missile had done its work. The mission had gone well until Lieutenant Jones and Lieutenant Slade spotted a SAM coming through the clouds. The pilot added power and turned into the missile which exploded near the Tomcat's tail. The fighter went into a spin as its crew fought to regain control.

By 13,000 feet, both men knew that they would not be able to stop the spin. While both aviators had decided to eject, Lieutenant Jones pulled the secondary handle first, sending his RIO, then himself, into the cold, black night.

The last time the two men saw each other was before they entered the clouds. Lieutenant Slade was captured within four hours and interned in Baghdad. He was repatriated at the end of the war.

Lieutenant Jones, however, was eventually rescued after eight hours on the ground, deep inside enemy territory. What follows is the story of those eight hours.

As he descended in his chute, Lieutenant Jones tried to pull out his PRC-90. However, because he normally flew without gloves, his hands were cold and he became afraid that he would drop his radio, even though it was tied to his vest. He knew his radio would be a vital survival tool on the ground and he pushed it back into its pocket.

"I had learned," he said, *"not to try to make a call in the cold air above 10,000 feet. Wait until you get down to a warmer area, below 8,000 feet."*

Lieutenant Jones landed and after stuffing his chute under his seatpan, took stock of his situation.

Here I was, down on the ground, inside Iraq. I could see where my Tomcat crashed from the ball of flames. I estimate that I came down 5-8 miles north of the site.

I started walking east. I'd like to say I did that to fool the Iraqis, but it was really out of confusion. (It was the first time I'd been shot down, after all.) Obviously, checking the terrain, looking for my RIO, trying to get him on the radio, in the dark, was confusing. I decided, finally, that it was time to move and I tried to get my bearings.

I looked at the smoke at the crash site. All the winds had been out of the west, so I tried to use the wind direction as a guide. Unfortunately, the winds were from the east. The horizon was only just starting to glow and I couldn't see the sun yet.

So, I began walking toward what I thought was the west. All the briefs told us to walk southwest for SAR, toward the Saudi border. I thought I was moving west, away from the Iraqi airfield we had attacked. As the sun came up, however, I realized my mistake.

I took my helmet off because It had reflective tape, but I couldn't bury it because the ground was so hard. My primary objective was to get as far away from my plane as I could. With the sun coming up, I wasn't thinking rescue, only evasion.

I used my helmet to "canoe" out some dirt and put dirt around it, ripping the visor off since it would glint in the sun. I knew the Iraqis would find me if they made an effort, but I thought hiding my helmet might buy a little time.

I was also very aware that I was leaving footprints everywhere because of the soft layer of dust over the main hard-packed earth. I could also see fresh footprints and tire tracks, residue from campfires, animal footprints, and debris. I kept looking for places to stop, but there was nothing, no mounds, no hills.

Finally, I came to a little vegetation, small bushes, really, and a few small mounds. I thought the only chance I had was to try to dig into one of those mounds and hide. I walked for two-and-a-half hours before I decided that there was nothing that would help me. I had expected helos to be in the air looking for me, at least by first light. But I hadn't seen or heard anything.

After an hour of laborious digging with his survival knife, he had scooped out a foxhole large enough to hide in. As he settled into his refuge, he saw a small truck approaching a blue, cylindrical tank. Two Iraqi farmers got out but did not see the American. By now it was 1205. He had been down for nearly six hours. He tried his radio again and heard American voices.

To my surprise someone came back with my callsign.

"Slate 46, how do you read?" he called.

That was the first time that I knew that there had been an ongoing SAR effort. I started thinking real fast. Anyway, someone started talking to me.

I was having reception trouble, mainly range, I guess.

Whenever I thought about the big picture, where I was, it would mortify me. As long as I kept taking it one step at a time, I was OK. It's like a combat mission or flying the ball. If you think about the big picture, if you're scared about getting a no-grade or a waveoff, you're not thinking about the mission or what you need to be doing.

"Let me come a little closer so I can talk to you," he said.

That was a real boost, but, I wondered who was this guy? Did we have Pave-Low-equipped helos out here? Were the SEALs out here?

He got DF cuts on me, using voice counts. I thought he was in the air, but I didn't know what type of airplane or where he was. Suddenly, I heard him.

"OK," he said, "I'll pickle a flare." He asked me where I was relative to my plane's crash site. Of course, this was after we'd gone through our authentication procedures. Everyone asks me if I cross-authenticated him. No! I dare anyone else to have enough presence of mind to do that. What would I say? "No, don't come and get me!" I'd rather sit out here and starve to death, or maybe become a POW."

He was coming north. "Look at your south," he told me. "I'll pickle a flare."

"I understand you're a helicopter," I said, trying to find out what type of plane he was.

"Negative," he said quickly. "I'm at 18,000 feet." Who would be way up there, I thought? He pickled the flare but I couldn't see him. He passed me, heading north, and shot off another flare. This time I saw it.

"Ok, now, I'll come down to where you can see me," he said. Lo and behold, he was an A-10!

He was Sandy 57, like those guys in Vietnam, trained in combat SAR. I brought him in with standard aviator talk. He didn't see me, but he flew right over me at 50-100 feet and dropped a waypoint in his INS.

"I've got to get some gas," he called. "Minimize your transmissions and come back up in 30 minutes." He headed south to the tanker track just south of the border. I found out later that he was also talking to the helicopters. They had been up from 0600-0900 looking for us, but had given up because it was getting too bright.

The Sandy pilot directed the helicopters toward Lieutenant Jones. As the SAR force headed for the downed Naval Aviator, they heard MiGs being vectored toward them. An F-15 RESCAP chased the threat away. After they got their gas, the A-10s returned, caught up with the helos and brought them in.

In the meantime, I had seen another farmer's truck headed in my direction, right at me. He hadn't seen me, but my heart didn't know that. They drove right past me, about 30-40 yards away, but didn't see me. They would have had to be actually looking for me.

As the truck went over the horizon, I heard the A-10s talking to the helicopters telling them they had another 30 miles to my position. The helos were actually on the ground, waiting for the Sandys to clear the way for them.

They asked me to shine my signal mirror south, which I did, but they didn't see it. Then, one of the A-10s told me to start looking for a helo about 15 miles out. As I looked south at standard helo altitudes—maybe 500 feet—I couldn't see them. But I did get a tally on the A-10s flying in a circle. I talked them in.

I had made a mistake earlier when I first contacted the Sandys. They asked me where I was relative to my plane's crash site.

"About 8-10 miles north," I replied. "About 1,000 yards due east of a blue tank." The Iraqis must have been listening to our transmissions, and, of course, they must have known where the tank was.

So, as the planes came in, and everything seemed to be heading to a big crescendo, about half a mile down the south road, I spotted a truck, an army truck, with the canvas covers—a grunt truck. I think we all saw it at the same time because the A-10 called, "We've got a fast mover on the dirt road." This guy was boresighting right at me, down in my hole. I saw a lot of dust and I thought I actually saw two trucks. We'll have to figure that out later.

I had a moment of panic there. But, hey—the A-10s have those huge cannons, and the helos must have .50-cal. Within 3-4 seconds, the Sandys set up a squirrel cage and rolled in on the truck, maybe 100 feet AGL, 200 feet slant range. They opened up with their 30-mike-mike. By the time they finished there was nothing out there, just flames and dust, about 100 yards from me. For the first time, I looked to the east and saw a helicopter, about five feet off the ground, watching the A-10s. I started talking to him. I had never seen such a beautiful sight as that big, brown American H-53.

He got about 50 yards away from me and I popped out of my hole for the first time. I grabbed my kneeboard cards and gear as he landed about 20 yards away. One of the special forces guys jumped out and waved me on. I jumped in and off we went, 140 miles to go at 140 knots, at 20 feet! Pretty impressive machine. Just what you'd expect from these special forces people with lots of guns hanging off them. As I looked out the back for the first time, 20-30 miles to the south, I saw the second helo. They had been flying cover for each other. Big spines on these guys, I'll tell you, being 150 miles into enemy territory during the day, in a helicopter.

After a brief medical exam at a forward base in Saudi Arabia, Lieutenant Jones got some food and tried to get a little sleep. However, a SCUD alert rousted him out of bed soon after he closed his eyes. The next day, an S-3 from his carrier flew him back to his squadron. Following a three-day rest, he returned to the cockpit.

Lieutenant Jones commented on his survival training.

There was a lot of luck, divine intervention, whatever. There's no way you can put Naval Aviators through SERE [Survival, Evasion, Rescue, and Escape] training, then dump them in a dirt parking lot, and expect them to evade without a little luck. An Iraqi helo could have just gone up and down on one-mile legs and found me—if they had made an effort, or perhaps, after picking up my RIO, realized that he came from a two-man plane. It wouldn't have taken them more than two hours.

My training at SERE School, though, helped me. My brain was going a mile a minute sometimes, but occasionally something would creep in from my training like, "Don't die of thirst with water in your canteens," or "Don't leave footprints."

Reprinted from the September 1991 issue of *Approach* magazine.

Far left above, two VF-32 Tomcats on the wing of an EA-3, which flew electronic intelligence missions throughout Desert Storm. *US Air Force.* Far left below, hardened aircraft shelters were easy targets for laser-guided bombs. *US Navy.* Left, the Air Force MH-53J Pave Low helo that rescued Lieutenant Devon Jones deep inside Iraq. *Craig Dugan*

Two Swordsmen Tomcats refuel from a KC-135. *Dave Parsons.* Right, Lieutenant Craig "Max" Dugan stands Alert 7 duty in the Red Sea wearing a desert hat. Alerts were stood in two hour increments. Two hours in the cockpit were preceded by two hours in the ready room as Alert 15, wearing flight gear as a backup to the Alert 7 aircrew. A well-equipped alert aircrew packs a Walkman (or portable CD player), writing materials to catch up on fan mail, reading materials for when the hand cramps from writing, a Nintendo Gameboy, an alert hat, and shades. *Craig Dugan*

View of al Qaim super phosphate plant in northwestern Iraq as seen over the shoulder of a Tomcat doing Mach 1.2 as it exits the area on a TARPS mission to assess damage on the plant from Navy and Air Force strikes. Al Qaim was a high-priority target due to its association with Iraq's nuclear program. The Iraqis valued it highly as it had four SA-3 and two SA-2 surface-to-air-missile sites protecting it, making it the most heavily defended target outside of Baghdad. *Dave Parsons*

Chapter 4

VF-11 Red Rippers

The Red Rippers trace their lineage to VF-5, which was established on February 1, 1927, at Hampton Roads, Virginia. VF-5 adopted the boar's head insignia shortly thereafter, although the name "Red Rippers" did not come about until the 1930 Chicago Air Races. The fact that the insignia bears a close resemblance to the Gordon's Gin label is no coincidence. From the start, the Rippers were extremely colorful and visible in the air and on the ground, developing a fierce comradeship that has been maintained through to today's Red Rippers. The traditional squadron explanation of their markings is, A Horny (boar's head) Bunch (string of bologna) of Two-Balled (design on shield) Bastards (slash on shield denotes illegitimacy).

The squadron was originally equipped with Curtiss F6C-3 Hawks and was part of the first *Lexington* air group, which brought a move to San Diego, California. For its superior performance during its first year, the squadron was selected to send a contingent to the 1928 National Air Races in Los Angeles. Red Ripper Lieutenant Junior Grade John Crommelin from VF-5 handily won the Navy Pursuit Race in a Boeing F2B-1 by pioneering a descending-pylon-turn technique that earned him a commendation from Charles Lindbergh.

The following summer, the squadron traded in their F2Bs for the beloved Boeing F4B-1, which they took to the 1930 Chicago Air Races where they were christened the "Red Rippers" in newspaper accounts of their aerial feats. At Chicago, they stole the show with a three-man precision flight demonstration in addition to their race participation. When a newspaper mistakenly referred to them as the High Hats (a rival Navy squadron, now VF-14 Tophatters), the VF-5 pilots were enraged. When the offending reporter asked the correct name, he decided the readership wasn't ready for "a horny bunch of two-balled bastards" and came up with the "Red Rippers." The name stuck.

In 1933, the Grumman FF-1 or ("Fifi") with its pioneering retractable gear began replacing the F2Bs. A year later, Curtiss F11Cs arrived to complement the FF-1s. In 1936, the squadron moved back to the Hampton Roads area for assignment to the USS *Ranger*. They received the Grumman F2F for a brief time before transitioning to the last of the great Navy biplanes, the Grumman F3F, in April 1937. All these aircraft featured a large Red Ripper design below the cockpit that became a striking and familiar symbol of the evolving years of naval aviation.

In late 1940, the Red Rippers took possession of the Navy's first F4F Wildcats, with which they would eventually see combat. When news of the attack on Pearl Harbor reached the Rippers, the squadron was embarked on the USS *Ranger* in the Atlantic. Eager to take the war to the enemy and avenge Pearl Harbor, the pilots presented the captain of the *Ranger* with a petition asking to refuel and rearm in San Diego and then take on Japan. They promised to "whip the Japs in sixty days." The Navy

The Red Rippers' boar's-head insignia is based on the design used on bottles of Gordon's gin. Left, a Red Ripper Tomcat heads toward the break with hook lowered upon return from mission at sea. Traditionally, carrier aviators lower hook during return to ship so wingmen can visually check each other for problems and make sure no one forgets to drop their hook and become the target of much ridicule. *US Navy*

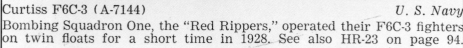
Curtiss F6C-3 (A-7144)   *U. S. Navy*
Bombing Squadron One, the "Red Rippers," operated their F6C-3 fighters on twin floats for a short time in 1928. See also HR-23 on page 94.

The Red Rippers flew F6C-3 fighters equipped with floats for a brief time in 1928, at which time the squadron was designated Bombing Squadron One. The boar's-head-and-shield squadron marking can be seen on the fuselage. *US Navy via John Elliot.* Above right, the Red Rippers flew the classic F4B-2 during the golden age of aviation with the boar's head prominently displayed on the fuselage. *US Navy.* Right, today, when it comes time for the air wing to spend time at sea aboard the carrier, it flies aboard over a period of several days while accomplishing carrier qualification. It didn't start out that way as shown in this picture. The original carrier homebases such as North Island and Norfolk all had airfields in close proximity so the aircraft could be taxied pierside where they would be lifted aboard. Here the Ranger air group, which includes Red Rippers in their F3Fs, taxis to the pier. *US Navy*

A shot of relaxed Red Ripper pilots taken in 1930. Note the crude boar's-head insignia design on the flag which strongly resembles the boar's-head design from the Gordon's gin bottle, which is not mere coincidence. Below, the Red Rippers flew the F2H-4 "Big" Banshee out of Oceana after taking their F2H-2 Banshees into combat in Korea. *US Navy*

thought otherwise and the Rippers were to see action against the Axis powers in Europe first.

The Ripper's baptism by fire came during Operation Torch, the landings in North Africa in the fall of 1942. During a four-day period, Rippers fought Vichy French Curtiss Hawks and Dewoitine D.520s, claiming sixteen aircraft destroyed against five losses.

After returning home for refitting and workups for the next deployment, the Rippers went to the North Atlantic in the fall of 1943, this time meeting the German adversary. The Rippers claimed a German Ju 88 and a He 115 off the coast of Norway. Returning home again in December, the Rippers began the turnaround cycle, upgrading to the Grumman F6F Hellcat.

In the summer of 1944, the squadron was directed to head west to Hawaii for their long-awaited crack at the Japanese. Assigned to the USS *Bunker Hill*, the Rippers flew their first Pacific combat in November 1944 with considerable success, earning two Presidential Unit Citations.

After the war, the Rippers operated the F4U Corsair. In August 1948, the squadron traded its Corsairs for F8F Bearcats and was redesignated VF-11. The F2H Banshee arrived in May 1950 and was to serve the Rippers well in action during the Korean conflict.

The first Red Rippers were disestablished on February 15, 1959. The next day, VF-43, which had been in existence since September 1, 1950, was redesignated VF-11 and decided to adopt the tradition along with the designation. The new Rippers converted to the F8U Crusader at the same time. Following a 1965 deployment, the squadron moved to Oceana for transition to the F-4B Phantom. VF-11 deployed to Southeast Asia aboard USS *Forrestal* in June 1967. Tragedy struck in July in the form of a catastrophic fire on the carrier which forced an early return.

The Red Rippers transitioned to the F-14A Tomcat in 1980 and made their first Tomcat cruise, aboard USS *Kennedy*, in 1982. The squadron continued to maintain a strong comradeship among its former members, conducting the most well attended reunions of any unit.

In the spring of 1991, the squadron was alerted to prepare to deploy aboard USS *Forrestal* to relieve USS *Roosevelt* on station off

The Red Rippers transitioned to the F-4B Phantom in 1965 after trading in their F-8 Crusaders. They then deployed to Southeast Asia aboard USS *Forrestal* in 1967 for a combat cruise. Below, a Red Ripper Tomcat in tension just prior to a catapult shot. The raised jet blast deflector (JBD) was specially modified for Tomcats by increasing the size and adding salt water cooling to counter the wide spacing of the F-14's engines and tremendous heat they generate. Far left, VF-11 Red Ripper tail design as it appeared in 1989 with the definitive squadron design on the tail. The squadron moved to NAS Miramar following the *Forrestal*'s last cruise in 1991 and began transitioning to the F-14D Tomcat. *US Navy*

Turkey, supporting Operation Provide Comfort. The *Forrestal* relieved *Roosevelt* in June and the squadron flew many missions to Iraq supporting the effort to protect Iraq's Kurdish minority group. In December, USS *Eisenhower* arrived allowing the *Forrestal* to return by Christmas. Upon their return, *Forrestal* was to become the training carrier based at NAS Pensacola, a move delayed by the unexpected Desert Storm carrier commitments. It was announced that its air wing, Carrier Air Wing 6, was to disband. VF-11, however, along with VF-31 were selected to move to NAS Miramar in the spring of 1992 in order to transition to the F-14D Tomcat.

Chapter 5

VF-14 Tophatters

Without question, the Tophatters of VF-14 are the oldest squadron in the Navy. Somehow, this one squadron survived fourteen redesignations without ever being disestablished and is sixteen years senior to its closest competitor. The birth of the Tophatters was in September 1919, when it was established as Air Detachment, Pacific Fleet, and equipped with the vintage JN, affectionately known as the Jenny. The squadron has flown twenty-two different types of aircraft and has been designated a torpedo, scouting, bombing, and fighter squadron at various times. A regular performer at national airshows, the "High Hats" were a household name and were featured in several movies before World War II.

The Tophatters were aboard USS *Langley* in 1926 as Fighter Plane Squadron One. When the United States plunged into World War II, the squadron flew off USS *Ranger* as VS-41. Teamed with VF-41 (the Red Rippers), the Tophatters flew their SBD-3 Dauntlesses on bombing missions in support of the Allied invasion of North Africa in 1942. In November 1943, they were doing business as VB-4 and flew the first American bombing missions against German forces in Norway in their SBD-5 Dauntless aircraft. The squadron saw action in the Pacific theater in November 1944, flying SB2C Helldivers off USS *Bunker Hill* during the Leyte campaign. In 1945, the squadron switched to USS *Essex* and was in action over Iwo Jima, Tokyo, and Okinawa.

During World War II, the High Hats also appeared on F6F Hellcats of VF-1. Fighting One was established in May 1943 at NAS Alameda, California. The squadron adopted the high hat insignia and called themselves the High Hatters, apparently unaware that the true High Hatters were still alive and well in the Atlantic. Fighting One went into action over the beaches of Tarawa in 1943 and from there were land based at Betio until February 1944. Embarked on USS *Yorktown*, VF-1 was in the thick of action during the great Marianas "Turkey Shoot," downing thirty-seven enemy aircraft.

During action in the Bonins one High Hat pilot was immortalized by his last words. Lieutenant Paul Pablo had been disappointed at not even seeing a Japanese aircraft on an earlier tour with another squadron in the Solomons. He was determined to make amends in the Bonins. He was last heard from in the midst of a swirling dogfight when he transmitted, "I've already got four, and I've got thirty cornered." Fighting One returned to the United States in late 1944 and re-formed for a last tour in 1945 aboard USS *Bennington*. By July, they were in action again over the Japanese mainland and were still on station off Japan when the war ended. In October VF-1 was disestablished, leaving the original High Hat squadron as the only squadron wearing the High Hat insignia.

Meanwhile, VB-4 was redesignated VA-1A in November 1946 and then again in August 1948 to VA-14. The final redesignation to VF-14 occurred on December 15, 1949, when the squadron entered the jet age flying the F3D Skyknight. In early 1950 they switched to the

The Tophatters' insignia has remained largely unchanged since the 1920s. Left, VF-14 Tophatter aircrews gathered for a photo during a cruise in the early 1980s. Note the tophat sported by the commanding officer. *US Navy*

The Tophatters were nationally known for their aerial demonstration team that toured the country performing aerial maneuvers while tied together. Note the tophat design on the fuselage. Below right, snappy wheel pants made the F11C-2 look fast at any speed. The Tophatters were a fighter squadron at this time. Below, the Tophatters traded their F3H Demons for the F-4B Phantom in 1963 and were the first F-4 squadron assigned to USS *Roosevelt*. In 1968, they joined Carrier Air Wing 1 aboard USS *John F. Kennedy*. US Navy

This Tophatter F-4B shows the classic colorful markings carried in the 1960s and early 1970s. The triple ejector bomb rack mounted below the Sidewinder launch rails is a Vietnam era modification that allowed bombs and missiles to be carried simultaneously. *US Navy*

F3H Demon. The Demon was traded for the F-4B Phantom in May 1963 and VF-14 became the first F-4 squadron to operate off USS *Roosevelt*. The Tophatters made a combat deployment to Southeast Asia in 1966, flying 967 combat sorties and delivering 651,624 pounds of ordnance.

The Tophatters came east in 1968 to fly off the newly commissioned USS *John F. Kennedy*. The squadron went back west to NAS Miramar briefly in 1974 to transition to the F-14 Tomcat at the West Coast RAG, VF-124. The Tophatters then brought their Tomcats to Oceana with VF-32 in 1975 and together made the first Tomcat deployment in the summer of 1975.

In 1983, the Tophatters supported Operation Urgent Fury, the liberation of Grenada. After logging combat over Grenada, the squad-ron journeyed to the eastern Mediterranean, where it logged combat time again in support of contingency operations in Lebanon.

In 1989, the Tophatters celebrated their seventieth anniversary. The distinctive, simple, and elegant Tophat promises to endure for seventy more.

In August 1990, the squadron deployed aboard USS *Kennedy* on four days notice to supplement USS *Saratoga* in the Red Sea as part of Operation Desert Shield. The squadron flew endless combat air patrol missions in the Red Sea protecting the fleet, and maintained training for combat that could occur at any time. Combat began on January 16, 1991, as Operation Desert Storm commenced. The Tophatters flew into Iraq providing fighter escort for Carrier Air Wing 3's attack aircraft. At the conclusion of Desert Storm, the squadron returned to NAS Oceana for a well-deserved rest.

A Tophatter Tomcat. *Dana Potts.* Far right above, a VF-14 Tomcat waits its turn while F/A-18 Hornets refuel from a US Air Force tanker. *Dana Potts.* Far right below, a VF-14 Tomcat during a cruise to Brazil. *US Navy.* Below left, as the Navy's oldest squadron, VF-14 was the first to be able to claim a seventieth anniversary, which occurred in 1989 and was proudly emblazoned on the squadron's two showbirds. *Dave Parsons*

Chapter 6

VF-31 Tomcatters

The Tomcatters have a long and illustrious history dating back to VF-1B, which was formed on July 1, 1935, flying Boeing F4B-4s. The squadron originally called themselves the Shooting Stars and was prominent in the fledgling days of naval aviation. Today the squadron is known as the Tomcatters and wears the symbol of Felix the Cat. The feisty Felix the Cat insignia was adopted during World War II and was so popular that it resulted in two squadrons being involved in a "cat fight" over its proper ownership. As a result, Felix was in use by two fighter squadrons from the summer of 1943 until the fall of 1945. Today, the squadron traces its lineage to the VF-1B Shooting Stars, but also carries the traditions of the original Felix squadron.

At the beginning of the war, Felix belonged to Lieutenant Commander Jimmy Thach's Fighting Three, which traces its lineage to 1923 when it was established as VF-2 and became the first squadron to operate from the USS *Langley*. In 1927 it became VF-6, only to become VB-2B in July 1928. In light of the switch to a bombing mission, Emil Chourre designed an insignia based on cartoonist Pat Sullivan's Felix the Cat. Chourre's Felix carried a bomb to mark the squadron's redesignation from VF-6 to VB-2B. The squadron was redesignated VF-6B in July 1930 and even though back in the fighter business, they retained the bomb in Felix's hands. At the time, they called themselves the Krazy Kat squadron. In the general reorganization of 1937, the squadron became VF-3, which corresponded to their assignment to USS *Saratoga*. As Fighting Three, they went to war with F4F-3 Wildcats under Thach's expert leadership.

Meanwhile, the Shooting Stars were alive and well, having been redesignated VF-8B during duty with USS *Enterprise*, which resulted in a redesignation to VF-6 in 1937 under the general reorganization. When the war broke out, the squadron was equipped with F4F-3 Wildcats under the command of famed Lieutenant Commander Wade McClusky.

Both Fighting Three and Fighting Six were prominent members of the "first team" in the Pacific at the beginning of World War II and fought together at Midway. Prior to the momentous Battle of Midway, Thach found himself ashore on Hawaii with an incomplete squadron (after losing twelve pilots to VF-2 in April) and without a carrier. Fighting Three's assigned carrier, USS *Saratoga*, had been struck by a torpedo in January 1942 and had gone back to the States in February for repair. When USS *Yorktown* returned from the Battle of Coral Sea with Fighting Forty-two depleted by combat, Thach merged his understrength VF-3 with VF-42 in order to have a full-strength fighter squadron for the impending confrontation at Midway.

Fighting Six was at full strength on the USS *Enterprise*. Both squadrons were in the thick of action against the vaunted Zero at Midway and earned themselves great distinction. Thach was able to field-test his beam

The VF-31 shoulder patch. Left, the colorful VF-31 markings are shown in this classic photo as Lieutenant Mike "Zone" Jones maintains perfect formation while flying inverted, one of his specialties. *US Navy*

defense tactic that ended up named the "Thach weave."

Both squadrons proved that superior airmanship and sound tactics could make the difference when the inferior Wildcat was pitted against the formidable Zero. Fighting Six stayed aboard *Enterprise* throughout the summer participating in Battle of the Eastern Solomons before going ashore briefly at Hawaii to refit in late August 1942. The squadron was in continual action until the summer of 1943, operating from USS *Saratoga* and detaching eighteen volunteers to augment the "Cactus Air Force" at Henderson Field on Guadalcanal.

On July 1, 1943, VF-6 was redesignated VF-3 and in late August returned to the States to regroup and transition to the F6F Hellcat. Upon the redesignation, Lieutenant Commander Lou Bauer decided to adopt the previous VF-3 insignia of Felix, apparently thinking VF-3 was no longer in active service. As a matter of fact, the same day VF-6 became VF-3, VF-3 became VF-6. Communications not being what they are today, the existence of two Felix the Cat squadrons was not discovered until later when the new VF-3 had grown quite attached to its mascot and therefore was unwilling to give it up. The dispute was only resolved by default when the new VF-6 (the original Felix squadron) was disestablished in October 1945. The Felix insignia was officially approved by the chief of naval operations for use by VF-3 on July 26, 1946. Since then, there have been no further "cat fights."

The squadron was designated VF-3A in November 1946 and began operating the F8F-1 Bearcat. The Felix squadron officially became VF-31 on August 7, 1948, as it entered the jet age, receiving its first Grumman F9F Panther. The squadron deployed to Korea in 1950 and in November downed one of the few MiGs credited to Navy pilots. After that conflict, the squadron moved to NAS Cecil Field and operated F2H Banshees, which they later traded for F3H Demons in 1956.

The mighty F-4 Phantom was graced with the Felix insignia in 1963, and the squadron moved to Oceana in 1965. During the surprise 1972 spring offensive mounted by North Vietnam across the demilitarized zone, many US carriers were diverted to the South China Sea to aid the South Vietnamese. USS *Saratoga* was scheduled to deploy to the Mediterranean with VF-31 aboard. Given seventy-two hours to

Officers of VF-6B, circa 1934. *US Navy.* Right, the Felix design was adapted from the Pat Sullivan cartoon character by Emil Chourre to carry a bomb. *VF-31.* Far right, one of the most famous aviators to wear the Felix patch was Lieutenant Edward "Butch" O'Hare who won the Medal of Honor flying a Felix-bedecked F4F Wildcat in the earliest days of World War II. *US Navy.* Upper right, Felix first appeared on the F-4 Phantom in 1963. *US Navy*

get under way, *Sara* made a "speedy" twenty-eight-day transit west, and engaged in heavy combat operations from May 18 through June 21; the squadron flew 490 combat and combat-support sorties. On June 21, Commander Sam Flynn and Lieutenant Bill John downed a North Vietnamese MiG-21 with a Sidewinder missile, which made VF-31 one of the select few squadrons that have scored aerial victories in World War II, Korea, and Vietnam.

After a long association with the F-4 Phantom, VF-31 transitioned to the F-14 Tomcat in 1980 and became a TARPS photo recon squadron. VF-31's traditional aircraft markings—black nose and red vertical stabilizers—were applied to the Tomcat, making VF-31 one of the most recognizable Tomcat squadrons in the community. VF-31 took their Tomcats into harm's way in 1983 while flying overland reconnaissance missions in support of the United Nations Peacekeeping Force in Lebanon. Very few squadrons can lay claim to such a long and rich history as the VF-31 Tomcatters.

In late spring 1991, the Tomcatters deployed aboard the *Forrestal* for the carrier's last cruise in order to relieve the *Roosevelt*, which was off the coast of Turkey participating in Operation Provide Comfort. The squadron flew many missions to eastern Turkey and Iraq in support of the effort to protect the Kurdish refugees in their post-Desert Storm exodus. Arriving back at Oceana in December, the squadron was selected to move to NAS Miramar in the spring of 1992 and become the first operational F-14D squadron.

Many inside and outside the squadron refer to this paint scheme as the "flying pencil," which some argue makes it too visible for air combat. However, strong loyalty to this scheme has kept it as the last of the colorful Navy markings. Chances are their newly received F-14D will not be as colorful. Below, a VF-31 Tomcat lifts off from NAS Oceana. The squadron began calling themselves Tomcatters after they transitioned to the Tomcat in 1980. *US Navy*

A VF-31 Tomcat is the center of attention at the 1990 Oshkosh airshow. *Greg Field.* Below, a VF-31 Tomcat caught at the moment of leaving the flight deck. The Tomcat has just gone from zero to roughly 150 miles an hour in less than two seconds. *US Navy.* Far left, Felix in a low-visibility paint scheme. The photo was taken just after the last cruise on *Forrestal* in 1991 and just before the squadron departed for NAS Miramar to begin transition to the F-14D Tomcat. *Joe Leo*

Chapter 7

VF-32 Swordsmen

VF-32 was established as VBF-3 on February 1, 1945, aboard USS *Yorktown.* In January 1945, the large fighter squadrons deployed in the Pacific were split into separate fighter (VF) and fighter-bomber (VBF) squadrons bringing them down to a reasonable size. Each fighter squadron had grown from a baker's dozen in 1942 to over seventy aircraft in 1945, with as many as one hundred pilots. This made for a very crowded ready room and was administratively too much for one squadron, so the squadrons were simply split in two. When the famed VF-3 was split into a fighter and fighter-bomber squadron, VBF-3 was created. VBF-3's complement included thirty-five F6F-5 Hellcats and fifty-seven pilots, most whom came from VF-3. Additional pilots came from VF-11 and VF-81. Lieutenant Commander Fritz Wolf reported aboard from VF-11 as the first commanding officer. His previous experience included combat as a Flying Tiger with Chennault's American Volunteer Group (AVG) in China.

The pilots did not like the "B" in the designation as it "implied a distinction, a step in the wrong direction toward mere explosive-lugging and bomb-dumping, which they secretly resented, according to the official squadron history. "Despite official directives, many a pilot quietly refused to add the dubious letter to his address—or, if he added it at all, he stuck it in after the F."

On February 16, 1945, a flight of VBF-3 F6F Hellcats were the first carrier-based aircraft to break through a blanketing overcast and attack the Japanese mainland. In their attack on Konoike airfield, they downed four enemy aircraft and destroyed nine more on the ground. At the end of a brief combat tour that concluded on February 25, the score stood at thirty-seven aircraft destroyed in the air and twenty destroyed on the ground. The squadron then headed back to the States to re-form, ending up at NAAS Oceana in July 1945.

In October 1946, VBF-3 completed transition to the F8F-1 Bearcat. The squadron was redesignated VF-4A in November 1946. The squadron insignia was a lion holding a shield under a pair of naval aviator wings. The mixed French and Latin motto *Dieu et Patria* was emblazoned on top. The motto was later corrected to *Deus et Patria*—Latin for "God and Country." Years later, a sword was added to the lion's hand.

The squadron was redesignated VF-32 in August 1948. VF-32 deployed to Korea equipped with F4U-4 Corsairs aboard USS *Leyte* on September 6, 1950, and was involved in extensive combat action. While conducting air strikes in support of beleaguered Marines at the Chosin Reservoir on December 4, a VF-32 Corsair was crippled by small arms fire and forced to crash-land. The pilot, Ensign Jesse L. Brown, was pinned in the cockpit and unable to extricate himself. Seeing the pilot's predicament while observing the aircraft in flames and realizing a rescue helicopter would not be in time, Lieutenant Junior Grade Tom Hudner force-landed his Corsair nearby, risking the same fate. Hudner survived the landing, ran to Brown, and put out the flames by throwing

The VF-32 Swordsmen squadron patch. Left, Gypsy 201 taxis at NAS Oceana wearing post Desert Storm markings. Gypsy is the Swordsmen's radio callsign. *Garry English*

F9F-6 Cougars of VF-32, circa 1953. Right, the Navy's first black aviator, Ensign Jesse Brown, was a member of VF-32 when it flew its F4U Corsairs to war in Korea. Brown's Corsair was hit by ground fire while supporting Marines at Chosin Reservoir and crash-landed his Corsair on a rugged mountain slope. He was trapped in the cockpit with serious injuries. Squadronmate Thomas Hudner force-landed his Corsair and tried to extricate Brown from the cockpit. Brown succumbed to his injuries and was posthumously awarded the Distinguished Flying Cross and later a frigate was named in his honor. Below, the Swordsmen gave up their F-8 Crusaders for the F-4B Phantom in the 1960s. *US Navy*

snow on them with his hands. Hudner found that Brown's leg was pinned in the cockpit and that Brown was lapsing in and out of consciousness due to internal injuries. He was unable to extricate his friend by himself. Eventually a Marine helicopter arrived with an ax, but Brown died as his rescuers worked to release him. Brown was mourned not only as a fellow naval aviator, but as the first black naval aviator. Hudner was later awarded the Medal of Honor for his actions.

In 1952, the squadron transitioned to the F2H-2 Banshee. Ground training began in March with the expectation of aircraft in June. When Banshees were not available as scheduled, the squadron borrowed three Banshees from VF-31 and VF-34 in July and checked all pilots out in them while operating their Corsairs. VF-32 never got its own Banshees, as a decision was made in November to equip the squadron with the first F9F-6 Cougars. The Cougars were adorned with large white lightning bolts edged in red, giving rise to the name of White Lightning. When the squadron received the first F-8 Crusaders in 1956, the new gray paint scheme did not lend itself to a white lightning bolt. The squadron initiated a contest to find a new name. During the 1958 Mediterranean cruise, the name Supersonic Swordsmen won. This was later shortened to Swordsmen.

Gypsy 200 in its latest CAG-bird paint scheme. *Dana Potts.* Lower right, Captain Tom Hudner USN (ret.) is reunited with VF-32 during a port visit to Boston in 1990, where Hudner serves as commissioner for veteran affairs for the state of Massachusetts. After telling the emotional and gripping story of his Medal of Honor winning flight, Hudner presented a model to the squadron of the F4U Corsair he force-landed behind enemy lines in Korea. Hudner was in turn presented with a flight jacket decorated with current VF-32 patches by Commander Bob Davis. *Dave Parsons.*

Chapter 8

VF-33 Starfighters

The VF-33 Starfighters are one of very few squadrons formed in the 1940s that have survived without redesignation. The squadron has, however, evolved through several name changes. The squadron was established in 1948 at NAS Quonset Point, Rhode Island, and equipped with F8F Bearcats.

Fighting Thirty-three subsequently deployed to Korea aboard USS *Leyte* in September 1950, flying F4U-4 Corsairs. The squadron flew continual ground support for US forces engaged in heavy combat at Chosin Reservoir. The squadron returned in February 1951 and transitioned to the F9F Cougar. After a Mediterranean cruise in 1954, the squadron moved to NAS Oceana and traded in their Cougars for FJ-3 Furys. In 1957, the squadron received F8U-2NE Crusaders and was assigned to USS *Enterprise. Enterprise* was called to participate in the Cuba blockade in October 1962.

In late 1964, the squadron turned in its beloved Crusaders and began to transition to the F-4 Phantom. At the time, the F-4 was still thought of more as an interceptor than a day-fighter, which was natural as previous squadrons had transitioned from F4D Skyrays and F3H Demons. VF-33's background in F-8s and day-fighter tactics infused new tactical thought into the fledgling Phantom community.

VF-33 received brand-new F-4Js in 1967, which they took to Vietnam aboard USS *America.* During the 1968 combat deployment to Southeast Asia, Lieutenant Roy Cash and Lieutenant Joseph Kain downed a MiG-21 with an AIM-9 Sidewinder missile, the first victory scored by an East Coast Phantom squadron. The squadron was awarded the Meritorious Unit Commendation for the combat introduction of the F-4J/AWG-10 aircraft weapon system.

From 1967 to 1971, the squadron was awarded both the chief of naval operations Safety "S" and the East Coast Battle "E" three times.

Returning from cruise in 1981, the squadron turned in its F-4J Phantoms for F-14A Tomcats. Following a short turnaround, their first deployment was in late 1982 and took the squadron to the Indian Ocean. In 1986, the squadron was involved in Gulf of Sidra operations, which included strikes against Libyan missile patrol boats and land targets.

The original squadron insignia featured a fierce tarsier monkey, chosen because of the tarsier's aggressive behavior and uniqueness as a flesh-eating monkey. The monkey was named Minky and had a fearsome face with stylized flames emanating from the side. The squadron briefly called themselves Astronauts while flying F11F Tigers. The aircraft were adorned with a bold yellow lightning bolt edged in black on the nose and top of the vertical stabilizer. The rudder was solid yellow with black stars. The squadron has used variations of this design ever since. Today their insignia is a single large star pierced by a lightning bolt. The fondness for stars is also reflected in a change of the squadron radio callsign from Rootbeer to Starfighter. By the 1980s, the

The VF-33 Starfighters' squadron patch. Left, VF-33 Starfighter Tomcat "hanging on the blades" during an Indian Ocean cruise in 1984. The tail markings are a combination of a lightning bolt, which dates far back into the squadron history, and the star, which evolved from Carrier Air Wing 6 (CVW-6) service aboard USS *America* during the Vietnam War in 1968. All CVW-6 aircraft were adorned with six stars on the tail at the time. VF-33 grew fond of the stars, modified them to one, and picked up the Starfighter callsign later on. *Dave Parsons*

VF-33 F-4J Phantoms over
USS *Independence.* Right,
a VF-33 F-4J Phantom
passes over the Wright
Brothers Memorial at Kitty
Hawk, North Carolina.
Oceana-based fighters do
most of their training over
the Atlantic Ocean to the
east of Kitty Hawk. *US
Navy*

squadron began to refer to themselves interchangeably as both Starfighters and Tarsiers. In 1987, the squadron officially revised its insignia to a Starfighter design and changed its name to Starfighters. Historical sentiment did not allow Minky to be banished forever, however. By 1989, junior officers got together and had small versions of the original Minky patch made, which they wear on their left shoulder.

The squadron deployed to the Middle East in December 1990 after an intensive workup aboard USS *America* arriving on station in the Red Sea the same day Desert Storm started. The Starfighters immediately flew combat air patrol alongside the *Saratoga*- and *Kennedy*-based Tomcats in the Red Sea and flew combat missions into Iraq the next day. In early February, the *America* was ordered to the Persian Gulf to join *Ranger*, *Roosevelt*, and *Midway*. USS *America* was the only carrier to see action in both the Red Sea and Persian Gulf.

VF-33 tail markings in 1991 show the definitive mating of the star and lightning bolt design. *Joe Leo.* Above left, a VF-33 Tomcat on the first Tomcat cruise in 1983 intercepts a Soviet Il-38 May over the Indian Ocean. *US Navy.* Below left, a VF-33 Tomcat on the catapult on USS *America*. *US Navy.* Left, a low-visibility Starfighter F-14 wearing the definitive markings that have evolved over several decades. *Dave Parsons*

Chapter 9

VF-41 Black Aces

The VF-41 Black Aces were established in September 1950 and are the fourth squadron to be designated VF-41. Assigned to Air Task Group 181, the squadron flew F2H-3 Banshees off USS *Randolph* in a November 1954 deployment. After cruises aboard USS *Forrestal* and USS *Bennington*, the squadron received F3H-2 Demons. The squadron insignia revolves around a black ace of spades. During their demon days, the insignia featured a stylized playing card character with a devilishly grinning face about to hurl a missile. This insignia was applied on a large, red fuselage band.

The squadron completed transition to the Phantom in March 1962, making it the third fleet F-4 squadron at Oceana. VF-41 deployed to NAS Key West—"hot pad," as it came to be known—between October 22 and November 22, the hottest period of the Cuban missile crisis. The Black Aces flew three times the average for an F-4 squadron during that time, intercepting unknown aircraft in and around the southern tip of Florida. During the early 1960s, they applied a large black spade on the vertical stabilizer.

The Phantoms were operated until 1976 when the squadron began transitioning to the F-14A Tomcat. The following year, VF-41 became the first squadron to carrier qualify aboard the USS *Nimitz*, which was to be its home until 1987. During the Tomcat years, the playing card character insignia added the Phoenix missile to his array of weapons. The aircraft markings were modified to suit the Tomcat by moving the diagonal red band to the

vertical tail where it bisected the black spade. This gave rise to a new, simpler insignia patterned on a straightforward playing card with a diagonal red band and a "41" in the center of the black spade.

The squadron performed the first successful multiple AIM-54 Phoenix shot by the fleet in 1979 when supersonic QF-4B and BQM-34 drones were both downed fifteen seconds apart. In 1980, the Black Aces were aboard USS *Nimitz* when it dashed from the Mediterranean to the coast of Iran via the Cape of Good Hope in eighteen days. The ship spent more than 100 days at sea during the tension surrounding the hostage situation in Iran and the aborted rescue attempt, which launched from *Nimitz*. VF-41 was assigned air support for the mission, which could have developed into a Tomcat versus Tomcat scenario if the Iranians had launched their own F-14s. To aid identification, *Nimitz* Tomcats were painted with special orange and black recognition stripes similar to those used by Israeli Mirages during the 1973 war. The squadron insignia was updated to a more modern and simple playing card during the Tomcat years.

In 1981, the squadron made history when a Libyan Su-22 Fitter fired upon a flight of two Black Aces F-14s. Recovering immediately from the surprise of this unprovoked attack, the two VF-41 Tomcats went on the attack and quickly dispatched both Fitters with AIM-9 Sidewinder missiles. This was the first combat use of the Tomcat by the US Navy and was immor-

The VF-41 Black Aces squadron patch. Left, a VF-41 Tomcat in low-level flight over the Nevada desert. *Bob Lawson*

VF-41 was an early F-4 squadron, transitioning to the Phantom at NAS Oceana after VF-102 in 1962. They immediately used the large tail surface to apply their ace of spades marking while adding a large red band across the fuselage. Right, for the Bicentennial in 1976, VF-41 modified the slashing red band on the tail into a red, white, and blue band. *US Navy*

In 1981, VF-41 made international news when two Black Aces Tomcats were fired upon by Libyan Su-22 Fitters. The Atoll missile fired by the Libyan pilot missed, but the Black Aces didn't and both Fitters were destroyed. The aircrews were Lieutenant Dave Venlet, Commander Hank Kleeman, Lieutenant Larry Muzynski, and Lieutenant Jim Anderson. All four received the Distinguished Flying Cross for their actions. *US Navy.* Above left, Commander Chris Wenthrich, Black Aces commanding officer (CO), addresses aircrews in the VF-41 ready room while deployed in the Persian Gulf. *Gerry Parsons.* Left, a VF-41 Tomcat low over the Saudi Arabian desert after the conclusion of Desert Storm. *Gerry Parsons*

Fine study of VF-41 markings during 1991 deployment to the Middle East. VF-41 CO Commander Ken Heimgartner modified the tail during his tenure in 1990 to the same design as the squadron patch, which resembles a playing card. *Gerry Parsons*. Right, a transitional tail design without the full playing card modification. *Joe Leo*

talized on thousands of posters: Tomcats 2, Libya 0.

In recognition of an outstanding year, the squadron won the coveted triple crown for 1981: the Battle "E," the Safety "S," and the Clifton trophy as top fighter squadron in the Navy.

In 1988, the Black Aces made the maiden cruise aboard USS *Roosevelt* and marked nine years of mishap-free flying. In the spring of 1990 the mark reached eleven years without a mishap, and the squadron celebrated winning the Battle "E" for 1989. As Desert Shield unfolded in late 1990, the squadron prepared to deploy aboard *Roosevelt* alongside *America* to augment the four carriers already on station. Leaving in late December, the *Roosevelt* passed through the Red Sea on the day Desert Storm erupted. At the conclusion of Desert Storm, *Roosevelt* remained on station until the area quieted down and then proceeded off the coast of Turkey to participate in Operation Provide Comfort. After relief by the *Forrestal*, the squadron returned to Oceana in June 1991.

Black Aces CO aircraft on the NAS Oceana flight line. *Bruce Trombecky*. Left, Lieutenant Steve "Wog" Carroll and some unknown hands clown around with models in the ready room. *US Navy*

115

Chapter 10

VF-43 Challengers

VF-43 has been the longest term resident of NAS Oceana, having taken up residence in the earliest days as VF-21. The squadron was created as VF-74A as part of the original air group assigned to USS *Midway* in May 1945. In August, the designation was changed to VF-74, followed by a change to VF-1B in November 1946. The squadron took its F4U-4 Corsairs aboard USS *Midway* in October 1947 for *Midway*'s maiden cruise. The squadron became VF-21 in September 1948 and transitioned to F9F-2 Panthers in the spring of 1950. The F9F-7 Cougar arrived in July 1953, and the squadron made a smooth transition to the swept-wing fighter as evidenced by the winning of the Battle "E" for that year. In 1955, the Cougar gave way to the FJ-3 Fury, and the squadron was the first to land aboard the newly commissioned USS *Forrestal* in 1956.

During this time frame, the squadron insignia featured a mailed fist smashing the word "Mach" on a background of blue and red stripes. At the time, the squadron referred to themselves as the "Mach-busters" or "Mach-knockers." In May 1957, the squadron traded in their F9F-7 Cougars for the F11F-1 Tigers. In November, the squadron was the first to take Tigers to sea when they operated off USS *Ranger*.

Prior to deployment with their Tigers, the squadron was given a total change of mission. As part of a modernization program of air group composition and training in 1958, VF-21 was made a part of a carrier replacement air group and given the role of F11F transition training. In November, the A4D Skyhawk supplanted the F11F Tigers. The Skyhawk training assumed precedence, since the Tiger was being phased out of service. The squadron added F9F-8T Cougar, T-33B Shooting Star, and T-28B Trojan aircraft to their inventory. The squadron provided all-weather instrument ground and flight training as the majority of tactical aviation was transitioning from prop to jet aircraft and emphasis on night and all-weather operations increased. In July 1959, the squadron was redesignated VA-43 in light of their switch to an attack-training mission. In 1963, their inventory included A4C Skyhawks and TF-9J/RF-9J Cougars.

The renaissance in air combat maneuver training that came out of the Ault report in 1968 resulted in the squadron flying occasional adversary missions in 1970. By this time, the squadron's primary role was instrument ground school and flight training and requalification. The adversary mission was added officially in 1973 when the squadron was redesignated VF-43. A supersonic T-38 Talon was inherited from Topgun in 1975, and four F-5E Tigers were added in 1976. A camouflage paint scheme was introduced to the squadron aircraft, marking it as an adversary outfit. The squadron modified its insignia to include a smashed MiG clenched in the mailed fist. Gradually the adversary role assumed more importance than instrument training and in 1978 the squadron's mission became primarily adversary support. In 1979 all instrument-training responsibility passed to

The VF-43 Challengers squadron patch. Left, in 1976, VF-43 added four F-5E Tigers to their inventory of A-4 Skyhawks. This gave the squadron a supersonic adversary aircraft similar in performance and size to the MiG-21. *Bruce Trombecky*

VA-45 at Cecil Field. At the same time, out-of-control flight (OCF), or "spin training" as it was known then, was introduced using the T-2C Buckeye.

The squadron pioneered the Fleet Fighter Air Combat Maneuvering Readiness Program (FFARP), an intensive three-week syllabus that includes a series of lectures followed by flights, which became standard for all fighter squadrons on both coasts. This program was initiated in 1978 and is now a part of every fleet F-14 squadron's turnaround training cycle.

In 1985, the squadron gave up its F-5Es and received Israeli F-21 Kfirs. The Kfirs were stood down in April 1988 as the squadron awaited delivery of the F-16N Falcon. The squadron began using the Falcon in June 1988. In late 1989, the F-5E Tiger returned to VF-43 as well, giving the squadron a variety of dissimilar aircraft. The squadron is never without "customers" and performs a crucial role in keeping F-14 aircrews honed to a high state of air-combat readiness.

Top, VF-43 traces its lineage to VF-21, a top East Coast F9F Cougar squadron that flew out of NAS Oceana in its earliest days. Above, the squadron became VA-43 in 1959 and was equipped with A4D Skyhawks. At the time, the squadron was assigned a training role for both the F11F Tiger and the Skyhawk and began acquiring other aircraft in its role as a RAG. Right, VF-43 Skyhawks in the hold-short area await clearance for takeoff for an ACM mission with these F-4 Phantoms. *US Navy*

Above left, a VF-43 Skyhawk being towed on the NAS Oceana flight line. *US Navy*. Above, the adversary lineup in 1986 included (front to back) the F-23 Kfir, the A-4E, A-4F, and TA-4J Skyhawk, and the T-2C Buckeye. The T-2C was used solely for spin training for Oceana-based aircrews. *Bruce Trombecky*. Left, VF-43 received the F-16N in 1988 after losing their Kfirs the previous year. The F-16N is the definitive adversary, capable of simulating radar, turn, and acceleration characteristics of the latest threat aircraft. *Bruce Trombecky*

Chapter 11

VF-74 Be-Devilers

The VF-74 Be-Devilers trace their origin to 1945 when they were created as VBF-20. Subsequently, the squadron was redesignated VF-10A in 1946 followed by VF-92 in 1949. In 1950, they were redesignated VF-74. The Be-Devilers took their F4U-4 Corsairs to Korea in May 1951 aboard USS *Bon Homme Richard*. The squadron was the last to give up the F4U Corsair.

In the post-Korean period, the squadron transitioned to the F4D Skyray. Although the Skyray climbed like nothing else, it achieved this high performance at the price of short range. Aerial refueling was just what was needed, but it was in its infancy for carrier aviation. Since it was still being developed, the Skyray had never been designed to take advantage of it as had the latest model A4D Skyhawk that was coming into service. An innovative pilot by the name of Lieutenant Jack Andrews solved the problem of limited range by fashioning a makeshift refueling probe by grafting a spare A4D refueling probe onto one of the Skyray drop tanks. Other Skyray squadrons followed suit as the Navy adopted the novel idea.

In 1961, VF-74 became the first Oceana-based fleet F-4 Phantom squadron. Prior to receiving its first Phantom, the squadron competed for the Bendix trophy, which honors the fastest coast-to-coast time. Commander Julian S. Lake, commanding officer of VF-74, served as officer in charge for the race against the clock. Two VF-74 crews competed, borrowing F4Hs from VF-101 Det A. Four Phantoms launched from Ontario, California, on May 24, 1961, each attempting to set the record to New York. When he landed three hours and three minutes later, Commander Lake had broken the record. His success was short-lived when fourteen minutes later, another Phantom landed after two hours and forty-seven minutes of flight. This established a new world record. Soon after, VF-74 completed transition and received their own complement of Phantoms.

When the squadron finally parted with the Phantom in 1983, VF-74 set the all-time record for any squadron operating a single type of fighter: twenty-two years. They could truly claim to be first and last in Phantoms for the Navy fleet fighter community. When VF-74 parted with the Phantom in 1983, they transitioned to the Tomcat.

In 1985, VF-74 Tomcats were part of the aerial interception of an EgyptAir airliner carrying hijackers of the *Achille Lauro*. Working with an E-2 Hawkeye airborne early warning aircraft, the Tomcats forced the airliner to land at an Italian controlled airfield where the hijackers were apprehended. A few months later on the same cruise, they participated in intensive combat air patrols in the vicinity of Libya's so-called Line of Death. VF-74 encountered Libyan aircraft in numerous aerial encounters in the first few months of 1986. In March, USS *America* joined USS *Saratoga* and USS *Coral Sea*. Libyan aircraft stayed away from the patrolling Tomcats. Instead, surface-to-air-missile sites lobbed missiles. Libyan missile-

The VF-74 squadron patch. Left, VF-74 Tomcats on the deck of USS *Saratoga*. The Be-Devilers flew from the deck of *Super Sara* to intercept the Egyptian airliner carrying the terrorist hijackers of the *Achille Lauro*, and along with VF-103, forced the airliner to land at NAS Sigonella, Italy, where they were taken into custody. *US Navy*

armed patrol boats were taken under fire on March 15, 1986, while *Saratoga* Tomcats flew cover.

In August 1988, the Be-Devilers became the first fleet squadron to receive the F-14A Plus Tomcat. Their initial cruise with the powerful F-14A Plus proved to be eventful as it occurred simultaneously with Iraq's invasion of Kuwait in August 1990. USS *Saratoga* went immediately to the Red Sea relieving USS *Eisenhower*. *Saratoga* was augmented by the USS *Kennedy* in September. As Desert Storm erupted in January 1991, the squadron was heavily involved in flying Red Sea patrol and escort missions into Iraq. The F-14A Plus was ideally suited for the medium to high altitudes flown and had no problem tanking at higher altitudes thanks to its more powerful F110 engines. As hostilities ended, the squadron soon departed for Norfolk, arriving in late March 1991.

VF-74 was the first fleet squadron to be equipped with the F-4 Phantom. *McDonnell Douglas*. Right, a VF-74 Phantom escorts a Soviet Bear D. *US Navy*. Above right, The Be-Deviler insignia on the tail of a VF-74 Tomcat. *US Navy*

Two VF-74 showbirds in formation. *Dana Potts.* Right, a VF-74 Tomcat refuels from a KA-6D tanker overhead USS *Saratoga. US Navy*

Chapter 12

VF-84 Jolly Rogers

VF-84 traces its name to the famous Fighting Seventeen of World War II fame. The original Jolly Rogers were formed on New Year's Day 1943 by Lieutenant Commander Tom Blackburn at NAS Norfolk, Virginia. Although Walt Disney-designed anthropomorphic insignia were all the rage, this new squadron wanted something less cutesy and more sinister. As one of the first Navy fighter squadrons to get the F4U Corsair, they settled on a skull-and-crossbones design befitting the Corsair name. The insignia was an instant hit and still conveys the original intent almost fifty years later.

The original VF-17 Jolly Rogers were disestablished on April 10, 1944, after a brilliant combat record. The executive officer, Lieutenant Commander Roger Hedrick, along with several VF-17 pilots, went on to form another squadron, VF-84, which adopted the Jolly Rogers name and insignia. During the Okinawan invasion, one of the squadron pilots, Ensign Jack Ernie, was lost in action. His last radio transmission was a request "to be remembered with the skull and crossbones." His family later presented the squadron with a set of skull and crossbones encased in glass, which, according to squadron legend, are actually those of Ensign Ernie. A time-honored rite of the squadron is the formal "passing of the bones" from one skipper to the next during the change-of-command ceremony.

The present-day VF-84 was established on July 1, 1955, at NAS Oceana. They were initially known as the Vagabonds and were equipped with the FJ-3 Fury. At the time, VF-61 was the Jolly Rogers. In 1959, VF-61 was disestablished and the Jolly Rogers insignia became inactive. The commanding officer of VF-61 became the commander of VF-84 and requested approval to become the latest Jolly Rogers. This was approved in April 1960. The fearsome skull on a black background was then applied to VF-84's F-8U Crusaders, which were received in 1959. VF-84 also retained a yellow band with black "supersonic" Vs on their side that were already in use. This merging of two designs has been continued through today.

The Crusader was traded in for the F-4B Phantom in 1964 for a long and successful association. VF-84 flew the F-4B, F-4J, and F-4N versions of the Phantom. Transition to the F-14 Tomcat began in 1976 and was completed a year later. The skull-and-crossbones insignia on the Tomcat's tail make VF-84 the most readily identifiable Tomcat squadron in the Navy. In 1979, VF-84 received the first TARPS pods in the fleet and pioneered the role of the Tomcat as a photo reconnaissance platform, taking the place of the RF-8 and RA-5 dedicated photo reconnaissance aircraft. The squadron achieved even more visibility after it played a prominent role in the 1980 movie *Final Countdown*. A dramatic scene pitting two VF-84 Tomcats against two Japanese Zeros helped make the Tomcat an international celebrity and VF-84 *the* squadron to be in. The squadron is far from being all show, however, witnessed by the winning of consecutive Battle "E"s in 1987 and 1988.

The VF-84 squadron patch. Left, a Jolly Roger Tomcat escorts an Italian F-104S Starfighter off the coast of Italy. The bold tail markings leave a lasting impression. Perhaps they are the source of communist propaganda that surfaced during the Vietnam conflict that called US pilots Yankee air pirates. The slashing design below the cockpit dates from VF-84's original markings when they were the Vagabonds. In 1959, the previous Jolly Rogers were disestablished and VF-84 adopted the Jolly Roger name and markings merging the Vagabond slash with the Jolly Roger tail. *US Navy*

This weather beaten F4U Corsair was known as *Hog 29*, assigned to Jolly Roger ace Ira "Ike" Kepford during the squadron's famed World War II combat debut in the Solomon Islands area. Kepford scored seventeen victories in World War II. Below, the Jolly Rogers insignia is the most sinister ever applied to an aircraft and the bold application seen here on these VF-84 F-4J Phantoms heralded the colorful era of bold and flashy markings applied to Navy aircraft in the late 1950s and continued through the 1970s until the advent of low-visibility markings. *US Navy*

In 1990, the USS *Roosevelt* was called to join the carriers already on station in the Mideast supporting Desert Shield. VF-84 readied themselves for combat in an accelerated workup on *Roosevelt* throughout the fall and winter of 1990. In late December, the call came to deploy and the *Roosevelt* headed east along with USS *America* on December 28. Both carriers arrived in the Red Sea on January 16 and were told that Desert Storm would commence that night. *America* stayed in the Red Sea and *Roosevelt* continued on to join USS *Ranger* and USS *Midway* in the Persian Gulf. Once on station, the squadron flew combat air patrol in eastern Iraq and later in central Iraq as the ground offensive commenced. The squadron also protected the fleet, flew fighter escort missions to Kuwait and Iraq protecting

the air wing's strike aircraft, and flew reconnaissance missions to gather bomb damage assessment.

After hostilities ended, the squadron remained on station briefly before proceeding to the eastern Mediterranean and Operation Provide Comfort, flying into Iraq from the opposite side. Jolly Rogers Tomcats were in the forefront of Operation Provide Comfort when they flew difficult night, infrared TARPS missions at low-level over northern Iraq. By the time *Forrestal* relieved *Roosevelt* on June 14, VF-84 had flown 111 sorties supporting Provide Comfort in addition to 468 combat sorties during Desert Storm. After being relieved by USS *Forrestal*, *Roosevelt* began the journey back to Norfolk.

A VF-84 F-4B Phantom hooked up for launch and about to go into tension. VF-84 traded in its F-8U Crusaders in 1964 for the F-4B Phantom. *McDonnell Douglas*

127

A time-honored Jolly Rogers tradition is the "passing of the bones" from the outgoing CO to the incoming CO. The bones are a prized mascot of sorts, closely guarded, and purported to be those of Jolly Roger Ensign Jack Ernie who was killed in action during the Pacific campaign in World War II. As he went down in flames, he made a last radio transmission asking "to be remembered with the skull and crossbones." Later his family presented the glass-encased skull and crossbones to the squadron. *US Navy.* Right, the Jolly Rogers tail markings are undoubtedly the most famous and recognizable. The movie *Final Countdown* brought the squadron worldwide fame, and for quite some time, every replacement in the RAG and student in training command wanted to be in VF-84. This era was particularly good for the Jolly Rogers as evidenced by the "E" with a slash mark denoting second consecutive award of the Battle "E." *Joe Leo*

128

A Jolly Roger Tomcat hurtles down the waist cat of USS *Nimitz* in full afterburner. Except in light fuel load conditions, all F-14A catapult launches are taken in full afterburner, which results in spectacular visual displays. *US Navy.* Below left, two Jolly Roger Tomcats fly formation with two Black Ace Tomcats. *Bob Lawson*

Chapter 13

VF-101 Grim Reapers

The Grim Reapers were formed in the spring of 1942 by the legendary Lieutenant Commander Jimmy Flatley. Flatley was fresh from the Battle of Coral Sea with two aerial victories and a Navy Cross. Along with Lieutenant Commander Jimmy Thach, Flatley was one of the most inspired tacticians in the fighter business at the time. As the first "Reaper Leader," Flatley arrived with a detailed fighter doctrine authored on the slow transport back from the South Pacific to San Diego. A natural leader, he took over VF-10 at NAS San Diego and forged the F4F Wildcat squadron into the famed "mowing machine" that would become the only squadron during World War II to deploy in Wildcats, Hellcats, and Corsairs. His fighter doctrine proved to be the ingredient for success against the highly maneuverable Japanese Zero that the Grim Reapers would soon face. With the motto Mow 'em Down, VF-10 sallied forth into the Pacific operating from island bases in the Solomons and off carriers.

Flatley took the Reapers into combat flying F4F Wildcats from USS *Enterprise*. The squadron joined *Enterprise* in October 1942 and sailed the Solomons area to join in the Battle of Santa Cruz, a pitched carrier-versus-carrier battle fought to protect the US forces in Guadalcanal. He was promoted out of the job into Commander Air Group 10, and as he left, advised the squadron to remember their lost comrades and upon meeting their foes to "rip 'em up and down, but do it smartly." The Reapers finished their first tour in 1942, refitted with F6F Hellcats in 1943, and returned to

combat in early 1944 aboard USS *Enterprise* led by Lieutenant Commander William "Killer" Kane.

As part of Task Force 58, which included nine aircraft carriers, VF-10 participated in the repeated strikes and sweeps against the Japanese bastion of Truk. During the first sweep against Truk on February 16, 1945, VF-10 shot down fourteen aircraft and flamed seventeen more on the ground. The skipper and his wingman accounted for five themselves. From February to April, Truk's air order of battle was steadily reduced from over 350 aircraft to barely a dozen. Task Force 58 proceeded farther into Japanese-held territory, and VF-10 was in the thick of the Marianas Turkey Shoot in June 1944. The squadron finished the tour and refitted with the F4U Corsair in preparation for a third combat deployment.

Joining Task Force 58 in March 1945 aboard USS *Intrepid*, the Reapers were in action over mainland Japan and Okinawa. April and May were the months of fierce kamikaze attacks. The squadron had its greatest day on April 16 when thirty-two enemy aircraft fell to their guns. Lieutenant Junior Grade Phil Kirkwood's division was responsible for twenty kamikazes in one mission. The star of the division, Ensign Alfred Lerch, downed six Nates (Nakajima Ki-27 fighters) and one Val (Aichi D3A dive-bomber) in that one sortie. Only one Reaper was lost. In thirty-four days, the squadron was credited with eighty-five enemy aircraft destroyed. The *Intrepid* returned to NAS Alameda, but before the squad-

The VF-101 patch features "Old Moe." Left, a Grim Reaper Tomcat flies formation with an A-4 adversary. *Dana Potts*

ron could return to the Pacific, the war had ended.

The Grim Reapers later became VF-101 and flew the F2 Banshee followed by the F4D Skyray in their last year as a fleet squadron. Under the "level readiness" concept, which led to the creation of the modern Replacement Air Group (RAG) concept, VF-101 merged with Fleet All Weather Training Group, Atlantic in 1958 and became the replacement group for the F4D Skyray and the F3H Demon. In 1959, the squadron began making preparations to add the F4H-1 to its replacement training. Lieutenant Commander Gerald O'Rourke was designated to be officer in charge of VF-101 Detachment A at Oceana and was charged with F4 training. O'Rourke led the first flight of Phantoms into Oceana on April 26, 1961. Detachment A fielded three teams in the Bendix Trophy race from California to New York in May 1961. In August, an F4H nicknamed *Sageburner* from VF-101 Detachment A set a speed record of 902.769 miles per hour. VF-101 eventually shed the F4D and F3H training as those types disappeared from service and moved the bulk of the squadron to Oceana. An air combat maneuvering training detachment was maintained at Key West, Florida, because of its superior weather for training.

In 1976, VF-101 became the East Coast RAG for the F-14 Tomcat, becoming fully operational when VF-41 and VF-84 began their transition from F-4s. The squadron maintained F-4 training until 1977 when VF-171 was commissioned as an F-4 RAG. VF-171 also took over the air combat maneuvering detachment at Key West. TARPS training was added in 1982. The F-14A Plus was debuted by VF-101 in 1988 and VF-101 remains the sole A Plus RAG. (The F-14A Plus is now termed the F-14B.) Although Key West has been used continually over the years for detachment training, VF-101 moved toward reestablishment of a permanent detachment in 1989. Permanent spaces have been assigned and although funding has precluded a full-time presence, the Reapers routinely deploy there. VF-101 maintains the critical role in making East Coast F-14 aircrew combat-ready before reporting to their fleet squadrons.

A VF-101 Tomcat on the flight line at NAS Key West during a tactics detachment in 1989. The A-4E in the foreground belongs to VF-45, which provides adversary support for VF-101 during the detachments. *Dave Parsons.* Below left, the Grim Reaper on the tail has come to be known as Old Moe which stems from the original VF-10 motto Mow'em Down. Although the patch has always featured Old Moe, the tails did not sport him until the early 1980s. *Dave Parsons.* Far left top, the first Phantoms to arrive at NAS Oceana belonged to VF-101 Detachment Alpha (Det A) which reported to the parent unit VF-101 at NAS Key West where it trained pilots to fly the F3H Demon and F4D Skyray. Det A had sole responsibility to create the RAG training syllabus for the new F4H-1 Phantom (redesignated the F-4B in 1962). *US Navy.* Far left center, after the F3H Demon and the F4D Skyray left the inventory, the Phantom became VF-101's sole responsibility. The Det A marking disappeared and the parent administration moved to NAS Oceana. The squadron maintained a detachment at NAS Key West for ACM training. The detachment had its own F-4 Phantoms that could be distinguished by their horizontally painted rudder stripes. *US Navy.* Far left bottom, VF-101 took on F-14 Tomcat training responsibilities in 1976. Here, a VF-101 Tomcat heads toward the vast training areas east of Oceana for a RAG syllabus flight. *Dave Parsons*

Chapter 14

VF-102 Diamondbacks

The Diamondbacks were established at NAS Cecil Field, Florida, in July 1955 and equipped with F2H-4 Banshees. The squadron chose a diamondback rattlesnake wrapped around the world as their symbol. The initial motto was Every Man a Ball of Fire. To give the pilots the necessary radar skills, an F3D Skyknight, with the Banshee radar installed, was also assigned. After one cruise aboard USS *Randolph,* the squadron turned in their "Banjos" for the F4D Skyray.

In 1958, the squadron received an invitation to visit Ross Allen's Reptile Institute to see some real diamondback rattlers. After dining on rattlesnake meat, Allen gave the squadron a mounted diamondback rattler as a mascot, as well as a stockpile of rattlesnake meat. After that, all new members as well as their spouses were required to eat rattlesnake meat as part of initiation into the squadron. The mascot acquired the name of Zap and he remains with the squadron to this day. In June 1959, the squadron moved their Skyrays to NAS Oceana as part of the master jet base relocation plan.

In 1961, the squadron became the second East Coast unit to transition to the F4H Phantom. The Diamondbacks flew aboard USS *Enterprise* and flew the first Phantoms over the Mediterranean.

In 1964, the squadron made the well-publicized around-the-world cruise in *Enterprise*'s Nuclear Task Force. Returning to the East Coast, the Diamondbacks were assigned to newly commissioned USS *America* in 1966. The squadron's outstanding performance was

recognized by the award of the Atlantic Fleet Battle "E" for 1964 and 1966. The squadron went west again in 1968 for a combat deployment to Vietnam after receiving the latest F-4J model of the Phantom.

During the 1970s, the Diamondbacks deployed in USS *Independence*. The squadron was on hand for the Jordanian crisis in 1970, earning a Meritorious Unit Citation. Other highlights included cross-deck operations aboard HMS *Ark Royal* in 1975 and 1978 and sorties above the Arctic Circle.

The Diamondbacks operated the F-4 Phantom for twenty years. After the last deployment aboard *Independence* in 1981, it began the transition to the F-14 Tomcat. Assigned the photo reconnaissance mission right out of the blocks, the squadron won the Tac Recce Award as the Navy's top TARPS East Coast squadron for 1982-83. In 1983, the squadron made a clean sweep of all categories in the VF-101 Reaper Recce Roundup competition.

The Diamondbacks made arduous deployments to the Indian Ocean in 1983 and 1984, remaining at sea for more than 100 days. In 1986, the squadron was in the thick of combat action in the Gulf of Sidra during March, providing combat air patrol around the clock for an extended period of time. During the subsequent raid on Libya in April, Diamondbacks were airborne before, during, and after the strikes, providing combat air patrol.

The squadron won the Tac Recce Award for 1985-86 and was selected to compete in the US Air Force-sponsored international Reconnais-

The VF-102 squadron patch. Left, VF-102 markings as they appeared in 1986, before the recent change of tail markings. This Tomcat is en route to the Tactical Aircrew Combat Training System (TACTS) range located just east of Cape Hatteras, North Carolina, and fifteen minutes by Tomcat from NAS Oceana. *Dave Parsons*

Right, VF-102 was established in 1955 and equipped with F2H-4 Banshees (known as the Big Banshee or Banjo). At the time, all Navy aircraft still carried the dark blue paint originated in World War II. In 1957, the Navy began repainting its aircraft in Gull Gray. *National Archives.* Above, VF-102 took their Banshees to sea aboard USS *Randolph.* Note the mix of gray and blue paint jobs that appeared during the transition period in the mid to late 1950s. *US Navy*

Left, the switch to gray
paint also heralded the
beginning of flashy paint
schemes on Navy aircraft.
Diamondback Skyrays
sported flashy red fuselage
spines festooned with
white diamonds. *US Navy.*
Above, the Diamondbacks
traded in their Skyrays for
Phantoms in 1961.
McDonnell Douglas

sance Air Meet 86 at Bergstrom Air Force Base, Texas, in October 1986 and again in 1988.

In 1990, the Diamondbacks were drawn into the allied coalition of forces against Iraq when the USS *America* was alerted to prepare to join USS *Kennedy*, USS *Saratoga*, USS *Midway*, and USS *Ranger* in the Red Sea in late December. An extensive and rapid workup ensued throughout the fall of 1990 to ready Carrier Air Wing 1 for possible combat. In late December, *America* and USS *Roosevelt* left Norfolk and headed east. Both carriers arrived in the Red Sea on the eve of Desert Storm. *America* stayed in the Red Sea while *Roosevelt* continued on to the Persian Gulf. The Diamondbacks quickly joined forces with their fellow Tomcat squadrons on the *Kennedy* and *Saratoga* flying combat air patrol, fighter escort into Iraq, and reconnaissance missions. In early February, *America* was ordered to the Persian Gulf to augment the three carriers already there in preparation for the ground offensive. The Diamondbacks received an extra TARPS pod from VF-32 on *Kennedy*, giving them four TARPS aircraft and pods to meet the heavy demands for photo reconnaissance in the Persian Gulf arena. The Diamondbacks had the distinction of flying missions into Iraq from both the Red Sea and Persian Gulf. At the conclusion of hostilities, *America* headed home after the departure of *Saratoga* and *Kennedy*.

Barely catching their breath after arriving in April, the squadron began working up for deployment again. An accelerated turnaround training program rushed the squadron through the full workup cycle and heading back to sea in late August, they sailed eastward to the North Sea for exercise North Star '91, Advanced Phase, and FleetEx. The squadron received the 1990 Grand Slam Award as the top F-14 or F/A-18 squadron for missile-firing proficiency in the Atlantic Fleet.

The Diamondback wives make a visit to the squadron dressed like their husbands (well, sort of). The six-month deployments bring the wives closer together especially when the carrier is involved in a hostile situation. This photo was staged to send with the husbands' monthly calendar, which is posted in the ready room. *Dave Parsons.* Left, a VF-102 Tomcat banks away over the Nevada desert during the Carrier Air Wing 1 weapons detachment in 1985. *Dave Parsons.* Far left above, in 1989 VF-102 changed their tail markings to look like the squadron patch and changed the carrier name from USS *America* in small letters to a larger and simpler USA. *Joe Leo.* Far left below, the Diamondbacks had left the USS *America* in the early 1970s for duty aboard USS *Independence.* After the last Phantom cruise on *Indy* ended in 1981, the squadron began transitioning to the F-14 Tomcat and was reassigned to Carrier Air Wing 1 aboard USS *America. Dave Parsons*

139

Chapter 15

VF-103 Sluggers

The VF-103 Sluggers date from 1952 when they flew the F4U Corsair. After a few years with the F9F Cougar, the Sluggers became one of the early F8U-1 Crusader squadrons. Once transitioned to the Crusader, the Sluggers joined CVG-10 aboard USS *Forrestal*. Teamed with VF-102 and their F4D Skyrays, the Sluggers were early innovators in demonstrating the tactical capabilities of the Crusaders, especially at high altitude. During the September 1958 Mediterranean cruise, the Sluggers turned the tables on the high-flying Royal Air Force (RAF) aircraft, which previously had been making unmolested high-altitude attacks on US carriers during allied exercises, much to the irritation of the US admirals. Until the advent of the Crusader, carrier-based fighters had been unable to get to RAF Canberras before they made their simulated attacks. Vice Admiral "Cat" Brown, commander of the Sixth Fleet, couldn't have been more pleased when *Forrestal* launched the Sluggers who tore into the Canberras before they could simulate their attacks.

The Sluggers made five *Forrestal* cruises, eventually moving up to the F-8E model for the July 1964 cruise. Since the earliest days, the Sluggers have marked their aircraft with a bold yellow arrow edged in black. The squadron insignia was initially a cloverleaf. Later a baseball bat was added, which stemmed from an early commanding officer who frequently carried one with him. This was embellished with a stylized aircraft darting from a cloud. Appro-

priately, the squadron radio callsign is "Clubleaf."

Before the end of the Vietnam conflict, the Sluggers began flying the F-4J Phantom. The Sluggers were scheduled to deploy to the Mediterranean aboard USS *Saratoga* in the summer of 1972 when the Vietnam War heated up. *Sara* was one of many carriers rushed to stem the North Vietnamese invasion. On August 10, 1972, a Slugger Phantom downed a MiG-21 Fishbed during a night interception. Lieutenant Commander Robert "Gene" Tucker and Lieutenant Junior Grade Stanley "Bruce" Edens shot down the MiG-21J with an AIM-7E Sparrow missile to score the Navy's only night MiG kill.

The Sluggers continued to operate the Phantom into the 1980s when most other fighter squadrons were flying Tomcats. Despite the age of their F-4S Phantoms, the squadron was the Atlantic fleet's nominee for the 1982 Clifton Award, which recognizes the top fighter squadron in the Navy.

In January 1983, the squadron went "back to school" at the RAG to transition to the F-14A Tomcat. Within a month of completing their transition, the squadron executed the East Coast's first low-altitude AIM-54 Phoenix missile shoot.

In October of 1985, the Sluggers were part of the Tomcat flight that intercepted the Egypt-Air Boeing 737 containing hijackers of the *Achille Lauro*. This dramatic counterblow at terrorism forced the 737 to land at NAS Sigonella, Italy, and allowed the hijackers to be

The VF-103 squadron patch. Left, two Slugger Tomcats in formation. In October 1985, VF-103 Tomcats assisted in forcing down an Egyptian 737 that held the hijackers of the *Achille Lauro*. Dana Potts

taken into custody; the episode prompted President Ronald Reagan to say, "I salute the Navy."

In 1989, the Sluggers completed transition to the F-14A Plus and were the first, along with VF-74, to take the Super Tomcat to sea.

In the summer of 1990, the Sluggers were preparing for a routine deployment aboard USS *Saratoga* when Iraqi forces invaded Kuwait. Departing for the Red Sea in August, where *Eisenhower* had already taken up station, the Sluggers became the first long-term residents of the Red Sea during Desert Shield. Working closely with VF-74 and the Tomcats of Carrier Air Wing 3 aboard USS *Kennedy*, the Sluggers developed and practiced the tactics to be used if hostilities developed.

When Desert Storm began in January, the Sluggers were in the midst of the fray, providing fighter escort to Air Wing 17 aircraft, combat air patrol for the battle group, and reconnaissance missions to search for Scud missiles and gather bomb damage assessment. The Sluggers proved the effectiveness of the General Electric F110 engines that enabled the F-14A Plus to enjoy greater performance than its F-14A counterparts. At the conclusion of Desert Storm, the *Saratoga* set sail for Norfolk, returning in late March 1991.

A Slugger Tomcat pitches into the vertical. *Dana Potts.* Above left, after a long and happy association with the Crusader, VF-103 transitioned to the Phantom in the early 1970s. They flew the F-4J model Phantom in Vietnam and came away with a night kill against a MiG-21. *US Navy.* Far left above, VF-103 used a stylized arrow as its trademark tail marking throughout its days with the Crusader, Phantom, and Tomcat, until 1991 when the squadron switched to using the squadron emblem on its tail. *Joe Leo.* Far left below, note the bright yellow helmets worn by these Sluggers. Designs on helmets are another place to show off a squadron's colors. Current regs don't allow paint and mandate a 90 percent covering by reflective tape, which makes detailing a flashy design a challenge. *US Navy*

Chapter 16

VF-142 Ghostriders

The Ghostriders were originally established as VF-193 at NAS Alameda in 1948 as an F8F Bearcat squadron. The squadron insignia features a cloaked skeleton wielding a bloodied saber atop a black stallion on a diamond shape. Initially the background color was blue. The squadron transitioned to the F4U-4 Corsair, which it flew during combat deployments to Korea in 1950-51 and 1952. During the first deployment aboard USS *Princeton,* the skipper of the Ghostriders made an important discovery while returning from a strike on the Kilchu bridges on March 2, 1951. He spotted a strategically located railroad bridge that occupied the best efforts of Air Group 19 over a thirty-day period against determined North Korean defenses until it was totally destroyed. James Michener heard the story of the epic duel (which came to be known as "Carlson's Canyon") during a visit to TF-77 and used it as the basis for *The Bridges at Toko-Ri,* the classic book and movie.

Following the Korean conflict, the squadron returned to NAS Moffett Field and transitioned to the F2H-3 Banshee. The squadron received the FJ-3M in 1956 and switched to the F3H-3 Demon in 1957. The Fury markings were a series of blue diamonds with no Ghostrider insignia on the aircraft itself. The squadron operated the Demon with distinction winning Battle "E"s in 1960 and 1962. The Ghostriders bade their Demons farewell in 1963 when they transitioned to the F-4 Phantom.

On their first Phantom deployment, VF-142 was on station in the Gulf of Tonkin aboard USS *Constellation* when hostilities broke out in 1964 and participated in the first strikes against North Vietnam. Between then and the end of US involvement, the Ghostriders made seven combat deployments. The squadron enjoyed considerable success against the North Vietnamese Air Force. They downed three MiG-21s, one MiG-17, and an AN-2 Colt between 1967 and 1972, making VF-142 one of the more effective F-4 squadrons. During the Phantom years, the squadron marked their aircraft with a yellow lightning bolt and alternating yellow and white striped rudder.

The squadron transitioned to the F-14A Tomcat in 1974 and moved from NAS Miramar to NAS Oceana in 1975 as one of the early Tomcat squadrons. Assigned to USS *America,* the Ghostriders deployed in 1976 and made the first F-14 intercept of a Soviet Tu-95 Bear.

During a 1980 deployment aboard USS *Eisenhower,* the squadron remained at sea continuously from April 16 to December 22 (except for one five-day port visit) due to the Iranian hostage crisis. The squadron was on station near Lebanon in 1983 in support of the United Nations Peacekeeping Forces in Beirut, resulting in another extended time at sea.

Initially, the yellow lightning bolt and striped rudder markings were applied to the F-14. When the squadron became one of the first with the drab low-visibility paint scheme

The VF-142 squadron patch. Left, a Ghostrider showbird takes on fuel from a VA-46 A-7E Corsair II while flying from USS *Eisenhower. Mike Silva*

The VF-193 Ghostriders took their F4U-4 Corsairs to war in Korea. *Robert E. Bennett via Bob Lawson*

Right, VF-142 was one of the successful F-4 Phantom squadrons during the Vietnam conflict downing three MiG-21s, a MiG-17, and an AN-2 Colt. VF-142 adorned its Phantoms with a bold lightning bolt in white, yellow, and black. Shown here are Lieutenant Commanders Gayle "Swede" Elie (left) and Robert Davis in front of their F-4 after downing a MiG-21. *US Navy*

in 1980, the bright yellow disappeared and a stylized version of the swordsman was placed on the vertical stabilizer. The lightning bolt and striped rudder design was dropped.

In June 1989, the squadron became one of only four Oceana-based fleet squadrons to be equipped with the powerful F-14A Plus. In March of 1990, the Ghostriders were one of the first two squadrons to take the A Plus on deployment. At the end of this deployment, the Ghostriders participated in the earliest days of Desert Shield when USS *Eisenhower* rushed to the Red Sea to take up station off the coast of Saudi Arabia.

VF-142 adorns its tail with a modification of its squadron emblem. This aircraft was one of the last F-14A Tomcats flown by the squadron before it transitioned to the F-14A Plus in 1989. *Dave Parsons.* Above left, a very unusual formation of Navy and Egyptian aircraft of US, French, Soviet, and Chinese origin passes by the Pyramids during Exercise Bright Star. Included are Egyptian F-4, F-6 (Chinese MiG-19 copy), F-16, and Mirage aircraft, a Ghostrider Tomcat, an A-7E, and an A-6E. *Department of Defense.* Below left, two Ghostrider Tomcats visit an A-7E tanker. The entire process is conducted with no radio communications, only hand signals upon join-up and departure. *John Leenhouts*

Chapter 17

VF-143 Pukin' Dogs

The Pukin' Dogs came into being as VF-871, a reserve F4U-4 Corsair squadron, at NAS Alameda in 1949. When the Korean War broke out the following year, VF-871 was called into action and deployed to Japan where the squadron flew aboard USS *Princeton* in May as part of Air Group 19X (relieving Air Group 19). The deployment ended in August with VF-871 remaining in an active status. In September 1952 the squadron returned to combat in Korea aboard USS *Essex*. The squadron continued to remain on active duty, being redesignated VF-123 in 1953 and equipped with F9F-2 Panthers. In 1956, while flying their new F9F-8 Cougars, the squadron conducted the first four-point aerial refueling from an R3Y-2 Tradewind.

Redesignation to VF-53 occurred in April 1958 and the squadron transitioned to the F3H Demon. As was commonplace in those days, the squadron abandoned its original markings and adopted the markings of a previous squadron with the same number. A previous VF-53, which had flown F9F Panthers in Korea as the Blue Knights, had an insignia with a winged black panther on a blue shield above the motto *Sans Reproache*. The new VF-53 adopted the insignia, but the name got lost in the shuffle.

The current distinctive squadron name came about quite by accident. Squadron lore has it that when the new design was unveiled, a lady (some versions say the skipper's wife) commented that the panther's head looked more like a puking dog than a bold mythologi-

cal creature. The name stuck and the squadron became known as the Pukin' Dogs.

The squadron was redesignated VF-143 in June 1962 and traded their F3H Demons for the Phantom. For many years, the Dogs were a Miramar-based squadron; from there, they deployed for seven Vietnam cruises. Teamed with VF-142, they were the first twin F-4 squadrons assigned to a carrier in advance of what would be common practice. A highlight of their extensive combat deployments was the downing of a MiG-21 in 1967.

The Dogs made the move to Oceana in 1976 after transitioning to the F-14 Tomcat. As a TARPS squadron, the Dogs flew the first combat TARPS missions as they flew forty-five reconnaissance sorties over war-torn Lebanon in the fall of 1983.

In 1989, the squadron transitioned to the F-14A Plus and became the first two squadrons (along with VF-142) to deploy with the latest and most potent Tomcat in 1990 aboard USS *Eisenhower*.

In 1988, the squadron name was the subject of heated debate in the pages of *Wings of Gold*, the magazine of the Association of Naval Aviation, after a Pukin' Dog pilot was featured on the cover with his patch proudly displayed on his shoulder. A subscriber wrote: "It is beyond me how any C.O. could approve such a patch as, Pukin' Dogs, or be proud to lead a group that would want to wear it." He went on to say he felt the patch was "sophomoric, vulgar and in poor taste" and that he hoped the "squadron and its leader are not

The VF-143 squadron patch. The Pukin' Dogs are notoriously fond of their mascot and heritage. This sign on the windshield of a Pukin' Dog Tomcat says it all! *Joe Higgins*

VF-143 MiG-killers Lieutenants Junior Grade Bob Hickey (pilot) and Jerry Morris (RIO) in their F-4B Phantom after downing a MiG-21 in 1967. *US Navy.* Right, the VF-143 CAG jet, resplendent in full color markings awaits its turn to launch onboard USS *Eisenhower. Joe Higgins*

typical of the modern Navy." There is no doubt that such a name today would not be approved under the current strict guidelines. But the Pukin' Dogs was grandfathered in and the squadron has held on to its unique name and will continue to do so regardless of external opinion. Suffice it to say that his comment elicited a barrage of support for the name by a few of the hundreds of former and current Dogs. After over twenty-five years of tradition, no leader or member of the Dogs would even consider changing their name.

When Kuwait was invaded in August 1990, the Dogs were deployed aboard *Eisenhower*, which rushed to the Red Sea to deter further aggression against Saudi Arabia. In late August, *Saratoga* arrived to relieve *Ike* and the Dogs headed back to Oceana, arriving in September.

The Dogs began turnaround training immediately and integrated air-to-ground training into their mission. During their Fallon Detachment, the Dogs became the first fleet squadron to drop live bombs, validating the F-14B's versatility as a strike-fighter.

The squadron was awarded the Atlantic Fleet Battle "E" for 1990 and proudly painted their markings on the F-4 Phantom gate guard at the NAS Oceana front gate. Later in the year, the first F-14 gate guard was moved into place and was christened with the markings of the Pukin' Dogs. The Dogs returned to the Middle East in December relieving USS *Forrestal* off the coast of Turkey.

A flight of three Pukin' Dog Tomcats heading home to NAS Oceana over the North Carolina shore. VF-143 moved to Oceana from Miramar in 1976 after transitioning to the Tomcat. *Mike Granler*

The Pukin' Dog mascot, referred to as the Dog stands near a VF-102 Diamondback Tomcat aboard USS *America* in 1986 while VF-143 was still ashore at NAS Oceana. Although the Pukin' Dogs insist that the Dog was kidnapped, the Dog has a different story to tell. Page 154 left, the Dog roomed in VF-102's eight-man JO bunkroom and grew quite close to his roommates during the 1986 combat cruise aboard USS *America*. Here Lieutenant Eugene "Geno" Miller bids farewell to the Dog as Lieutenant Steve "Surf" Dunwoody holds him. Shortly thereafter, the Dog crossdecked to the USS *Saratoga*, which was returning home, so he could rejoin VF-143, which was despondent over his absence. Page 154 right, the Dog looks out at sea from a perch atop a VF-33 Tomcat during his stay aboard *America*. The Dog chose this aircraft because the name of Lieutenant Commander Ted Spilman, a former Dog himself, was on the canopy rail. *Dave Parsons*

The True Story of the Missing Dog

Now, at long last, the truth about the saga of the missing dog can finally be told. On March 9, 1986 the mascot of VF-143, the famous Pukin' Dog himself, was missing from his cage in the Pukin' Dog ready room at NAS Oceana. Upon finding the cage empty and his chains slack, the obvious conclusion was some foul fate had befallen the Dog.

Meanwhile, at Pier 12 at Norfolk Naval Base, Carrier Air Wing 1 was in the process of embarking aboard USS *America*. *America* was scheduled to depart on the morning tide to join USS *Coral Sea* and USS *Saratoga,* which were already on station in the Mediterranean Sea off the coast of Libya. Rumor had it that once all three carriers were on station, the world would see how serious Moammar Khadafy really was about his Line of Death. The Dog was well aware of these rumors, since the VF-143 ready room was adjacent to that of VF-102, which had been aflutter the past week in preparation for the accelerated deployment.

VF-143, for that matter, had come to be known as the local "National Guard." The Dog hadn't tasted salt air in quite some time because the Pukin' Dogs had been shore-based for almost two years while the *Ike* was in the yards. Heck, if he had wanted to join the "National Guard" in the first place, he would have. Anyway, who wanted to be in an F-14 squadron on the beach when anyone who had seen the movie *Top Gun* knew something big was brewing in the Med with two carriers already on station off Libya and a third getting ready to join them. Besides, the boys in 143 were having a lot of fun at the club, but *was* the Dog invited? Heck no! He was lucky to get fresh water every day. Hey, a guy (or dog) can only take it so long in a cage and in chains. The squadron had just come to take the old dog for granted and hadn't even considered nor could they admit that the Dog had taken off on his own.

So it came as no surprise to those close enough to know or care when the cage was found empty. Some pointed fingers, some cried out in indignation, some smiled knowing smiles, and then there were the few members of VF-102's eight-man bunk room too junior to fly aboard. As the *America* slipped its lines the morning of the tenth, they awoke to find the stowaway Dog in their midst. How the Dog got there was anyone's guess as he offered no explanations or clues other than he was there to stay. The best guess was that he persuaded the officer of the day that he was the new drug dog to replace the one who transferred

out two weeks earlier due to nerves. As the *America* was now passing the Bay Bridge Tunnel en route to points east, it looked like the Dog would indeed get his wish.

The Diamondbacks' main concern was that the Pukin' Dogs might think they had perpetrated a dognapping, so they encouraged the Dog to write home or at least send a telegram explaining the circumstances. The Dog said the situation was "covered" so not to sweat it. However, the Diamondbacks' worst fears were realized two days later when messages began arriving from Oceana. The first read:

DEAR DIAMONDBACK JO MEATHEADS
GOOD JOB. REQUEST TERMS FOR
RETURN OF DOG SOONEST.

VF-143 JOS

This perplexed both the Dog and the Diamondbacks, for they both knew the Dog was onboard by choice. Heck, the Diamondbacks didn't harbor any grudges against VF-143, except maybe the fact 102 was flying tired Block 90 updates (reworked Tomcats that had been around for at least ten years), while 143 had brand-new jets that had never even seen salt water, but that didn't involve the Dog. Jokingly, someone mentioned that 143 should trade one of their Block 130s for one of 102's tired Turkeys as ransom. At any rate, the Dog was his own person, aboard of his own free will, so how could terms be discussed? The Diamondbacks didn't have time to worry about it with all the preparations for the impending operations off Libya.

Two more messages arrived from Oceana, an official one from the fighter wing and another semi-official one from Linda Lyle, the VF-102 skipper's wife, who had caught wind of VF-143's coverup and campaign to discredit VF-102. It appeared that the Pukin' Dogs were considerably distressed over the departure of their mascot and were pulling out all the stops to get him back. Refusing to believe that the Dog could have possibly left of his own accord, they had gone to the wing with a tale of abduction by scurrilous Diamondbacks in the dead of night who impersonated the fighter wing duty officer to lure away the Dog's guard with a false report of trouble on the flight line. They convinced Commander "Dink" Tillman, acting wing commander, that if nothing else, they were distraught over the disappearance to the point of being useless as an F-14 squadron. He fired off a message to the Diamondback skipper Commander "Sparky" Lyle, suggesting the Dog be returned at the earliest opportunity to end the brouhaha VF-143 was raising.

Meanwhile, Linda Lyle was beset by threats and innuendoes from the executive officer of VF-143 about the return of the Dog. She fired off another message warning her husband that his beloved Shane, a golden retriever, was a marked dog, and neighbors had seen strange cars in their secluded cul de sac bearing Pukin' Dogs zappers on the rear windows. Sparky answered the messages informing them that the Dog had appeared on his own and assuring them of the Dog's imminent and safe return.

In the Diamondback ready room, the junior officers got together to discuss what to do about the message from the VF-143 junior officers. The Diamondbacks were a little taken back at the inference that they had absconded with the Dog, but at the same time, knowing of the VF-143 executive's demeanor and the seriousness of his threats, surmised that the 143 junior officers were probably under the executive officer's gun to get the Dog back. They tried to get the Dog to send a reply to clear up the matter, but he was more upset than anyone else. He viewed 143's actions as an elaborate smoke screen to cover for the real situation and their shabby treatment of him. Understandably, he gloated over 143's dismay and wasn't going to do anything to ease their travails. So he and the Diamondbacks concocted a response to tease the 143 ready room which read:

FM DIAMONDBACK JOS
TO PUKIN DOG JOS

SUBJ "PUKIN DOG"
REF A FITRON ONE FOUR THREE
    121940Z MAR 86
    B COMFITWINGONE 122148 MAR
    86

OH WHERE OH WHERE HAS YOUR
   LITTLE DOG GONE
OH WHERE OH WHERE COULD HE BE
OH NO WE FEAR HE'S BEEN
   DOGNAPPED MY DEAR
BY THE DIAMONDBACKS OUT AT SEA
THE NATIONAL GUARD MAY BE FINE
   FOR YOU JOS
BACK ON THE BEACH DRINKING BEER
BUT YOUR POOCH WOULD RATHER BE
   HERE WITH US
PUKIN IN MOAMMAR'S EAR

DON'T WORRY, SAVE A SEAT AT THE FLING FOR THE "DOG"
TRUST US, THE DOG'S IN THE MAIL
DIAMONDBACK JOS

(The Fling was the annual "Fighter Fling," a gathering of all East Coast fighter squadrons. The Dog figured Khadafy would be squared away in time to hop a ride home on one of the returning carriers so he wouldn't miss the Fling in June.)

The plan from there on was to have the Dog cross-deck to the *Saratoga* when it turned over to the *America* later in the month. The Dog wanted to return with VF-103 due to the fact that the prospective executive officer of VF-143 was with VF-74 and he was sure the current VF-143 exec had gotten word to him to get the Dog. For his part, the Dog wanted to get back to Oceana to tell his side of the story without an "escort" under direction of 143.

The Dog managed to get aboard *Sara* and into a Slugger bunk room for the voyage back. Once back at Oceana, the ruckus cooled considerably when the Dog cleared the air. He still never got to see *Top Gun*; maybe the 143 guys were jealous of the Armed Forces Expeditionary Medal and Navy Expeditionary Medal he got while aboard *America*.

A lineup of VF-143 Tomcats with the famous Pukin' Dog on their tails. Legend has it that the design is a mythological creature called the Griffin. However, the first skipper's wife took one look at it and said it more resembled a dog throwing up, hence the name Pukin' Dogs. The squadron clings affectionately to the name, which has been a source of public debate over whether it is proper or not. It certainly would not be approved if submitted in today's climate, but the name has been grandfathered in, and there are too many aviators that have served as Pukin' Dogs to let the name be banished. *Garry English*

Index